STORIES OF AUTISTIC JOY

by the same author

Uncomfortable Labels

My Life as a Gay Autistic Trans Woman

Laura Kate Dale

ISBN 978 1 78592 587 0

eISBN 978 1 78592 588 7

Me and My Dysphoria Monster

An Empowering Story to Help Children Cope with Gender Dysphoria

Laura Kate Dale

Illustrated by Hui Qing Ang

ISBN 978 1 83997 092 4

eISBN 978 1 83997 093 1

of related interest

Queerly Autistic

The Ultimate Guide for LGBTQIA+ Teens on the Spectrum

Erin Ekins

ISBN 978 1 78775 171 2

eISBN 978 1 78775 172 9

The Autistic Trans Guide to Life

Yenn Purkis and Dr. Wenn Lawson

Foreword by Emma Goodall

ISBN 978 1 78775 391 4

eISBN 978 1 78775 392 1

STORIES OF AUTISTIC JOY

Edited by
Laura Kate Dale

Jessica Kingsley Publishers
London and Philadelphia

First published in Great Britain in 2024 by Jessica Kingsley Publishers
An imprint of John Murray Press

1

A CIP catalogue record for this title is available from the British Library and the Library of Congress

ISBN 978 1 83997 809 8
eISBN 978 1 83997 810 4

Printed and bound in Great Britain by TJ Books Ltd

Jessica Kingsley Publishers' policy is to use papers that are natural, renewable and recyclable products and made from wood grown in sustainable forests. The logging and manufacturing processes are expected to conform to the environmental regulations of the country of origin.

Jessica Kingsley Publishers
Carmelite House
50 Victoria Embankment
London EC4Y 0DZ

www.jkp.com

John Murray Press
Part of Hodder & Stoughton Ltd
An Hachette Company

Contents

Introduction

The Importance of Stories of Autistic Joy

Laura Kate Dale

Thirty-two-year-old author and autistic trans woman living in London, UK.

For those of us with a formal autism spectrum diagnosis, that diagnosis usually comes as a direct result of struggle, suffering, and impairment. Whether diagnosis comes as a result of a parent concerned we're not making social connections comparable to those of our allistic peers, or from our own experiences struggling to manage basic sensory data and changes in routine that seem to be so simple for those around us, a formal diagnosis usually means that someone was concerned that we, as autistic people, are struggling to live the same kind of life as those around us.

Even outside of the world of formal diagnosis, a world often gatekept by outdated gender-skewed diagnostic criteria and a history of underserving minority communities, the same is very much true. Those I have known in life who came to self-diagnosis often did so first and foremost because of the areas in their life where they were struggling.

That is obviously not a completely universal experience, but I think those kinds of stories are a big part of why, at the end of the day, so many stories shared by, and about, autistic life center on discussing difficulties and struggles in day-to-day living. When struggle is what leads to a name being placed on your lived experience, it's easy to let that define how you view things.

From the outsider perspective of someone who is not themselves autistic, autism is also often viewed and discussed through a lens of suffering. Oh how terrible it must be to live life overwhelmed by sounds, smells, and textures. Oh how awful it must be to live a life formed of rigid routine, repeated activities, and unchanging factors. Oh how painful it must be to not be able to connect with allistic individuals as easily as they connect with each other.

Our lives are viewed as miserable because, to the non-autistic observer, our lives differ from the template laid out by society. Our lives differ from the default, and therefore must be falling short of perfection.

When all you see of a person is the ways they struggle to assimilate, it is easy to assume that behind that experience is an inherently lesser life.

It may seem odd to introduce an anthology centered on autistic joy with several paragraphs about autistic struggles, but I am forced to be clear up front with this anthology: I am not unaware of autistic suffering. I am an autistic adult myself, one who has had to try and function for the past 32 years in a world that was not built to accommodate the way my brain works. There are days where a simple change in plans will spiral me into a meltdown that disables my ability to manage daily tasks, and days where my inability to communicate with non-autistic people clearly causes me distress and confusion that can be deeply upsetting.

Autism is a disability, at least when living in a world of non-autistic individuals, and I am not here to shy away from that with this book.

I acknowledge that a book centering autistic joy has to decenter, to a degree, discussions of autistic struggles. I do so, while not burying that part of the autistic experience. Autistic joy is complicated to discuss, in part because of the importance of not burying accounts of autistic disability and struggle, but also because of the issues with how stories of autistic joy are often forced into a voyeuristic mold by onlookers.

When writing a book about stories of joy as a disabled person, particularly an autistic person, this kind of preamble unfortunately feels necessary. All too often, stories of autistic joy are only allowed to exist in society today as part of a category I would describe as "inspiration porn." If you've not heard the term before, it's used to describe content where a disabled person living their day-to-day life is documented by an outside observer, usually someone not themselves disabled, and taken out of context for a non-disabled audience to stare at as entertainment. It is particularly prevalent around autism, with an entire genre of online content dedicated to parents viewing autistic joy through an outside lens, not interested in the interior experience of joy of the autistic individual, but instead infantilizing them, calling them brave, stripping them of agency, and removing their actions from the context of their lived experience. This kind of content is the direct and extreme antithesis to that doom-and-gloom view of autistic life, and it is deeply flawed in its own ways.

All too often these kinds of videos about autistic joy lean completely away from acknowledging that autism is a disability, and paint it purely as an amazing superpower that comes with no struggles whatsoever. You see this in depictions of savants, incredibly rare individuals with incredible unique gifts. You see it in patronizing posts about how beautiful it would be to be able to be autistic, from people who I suspect know they wouldn't actually enjoy living with a disability. You see it in stories that underestimate autistic people, to the point where even basic achievements elicit surprised responses, while onlookers heap on praise the way they would when proud of a toddler.

When first deciding I wanted to put together this anthology of stories of autistic joy, the balancing act for me was assembling a collection of stories that focus on autistic joy, but without erasing the fact that the condition is a disability, or going in the opposite direction and painting autism as purely wonderful to live with. I wanted to make sure I centered joy, without painting a one-sided picture of life.

A little background about myself: my name is Laura Kate Dale, and I am a published author and media critic. I am 32 years old, queer, and transgender. My memoir, *Uncomfortable Labels*, published back in 2019, focused on the intersection of living as both trans and autistic, and the ways that those facets of my life intersected and overlapped. When I wrote that book, a lot of my focus was on struggle and challenge. A lot of my life prior to formal diagnosis was defined by my struggles as an undiagnosed autistic person living without support tools or accommodations for my condition, and it felt important to talk about what was difficult, to help those who read the book to understand why I am, fundamentally, the person I am today.

But in the years since that book was published, and generally in the years since my diagnosis, my relationship with my autism diagnosis has actually changed quite dramatically. Sure, I still struggle with elements of my life as a disabled person, but I have over the past decade become a lot better at seeing, and articulating, the unique joys I experience, day to day, in life.

What I think sets this anthology apart is the fact that it is entirely a collection of own voices stories shared by autistic writers, which attempts to shed light on autistic joy through an unapologetically introspective autistic lens, focused on the minutiae of the ways we experience joy. In my own essays, which make up around one quarter of this collection, as well as the essays of our wonderfully varied contributors, we aim to explain experiences of autistic joy through a lens of subjective, internal, personal experience. My hope as this collection's editor is that for anyone reading who is not autistic themselves, each essay can give you some insight into the autistic experience that sheds light on why autistic life isn't entirely about struggling and suffering, and how the areas where we find joy, and suffering, are often two sides of the same coin.

From stories about the joy of sorting, organizing, and collecting, to stories about the unique joys of autistic socialization, the beauty of hyperfixations, and the freedom that comes from comfort textures, this anthology aims to show the autistic experience not as one that is always amazing and without struggle, but one full of small unique beautiful joys, as told by the people living autistic lives.

Suffering is a part of autistic life, but it's often not the focus, and in this anthology that is what I hope to capture. These stories focusing on joy are not erasing the fact that suffering and challenges come hand in hand with being autistic, but are aiming to carve out a space to explain and contextualize autistic joy, on autistic terms, from an autistic perspective.

These stories come from a variety of wonderful autistic authors with a wide range of support needs, from a wide range of different countries, and with a variety of different backgrounds. The essays were selected in part to ensure a variety of perspectives on the autistic experience, prioritizing giving space to those from backgrounds who face additional barriers to diagnosis, or whose stories as autistic people are too rarely given a spotlight.

For those of you reading who are not yourselves autistic, I hope you come away with some new understanding of the unique shapes that autistic joy can form.

How Pretending to Be a Magical Animal Helped Me Feel Human

Miles Nelson

Note: my favorite RPG (roleplaying game) growing up, the one that plays a large part in this story, is still active and has a small yet bustling community to this day. In order to preserve their anonymity, I will not be including the domain of the website or the names of any of its members.

Have you ever come home, hungry and tired, from a long day at work? Have you looked at your cat or dog sprawled out in a warm patch of sun, and thought, "I wish I had a life like yours"?

Well, that's quite an easy way to describe my childhood. Each day back then I would arrive home from school with my brain full of words and with ears ringing, exhausted and overwhelmed for reasons I could never begin to guess. Each day I'd slump down at my desk, curl up, and daydream of being someone else.

My name is Miles. I'm a transgender and autistic man from Durham, England, and for most of my childhood I felt inhuman.

From starting nursery, when I first began to interact with other children regularly, I was known as the weird kid who would ask to be the pet hamster when the other kids were pretending to be happy families. I purred when happy, and could perfectly mimic a barking dog. Every night when I was asleep, I dreamt I could breathe fire and fly (I still often do). Ironically, it was only then when I felt like my truest, most authentic self.

Back then, I was just a lost little girl. Something felt wrong, but I didn't know what.

So this is the story of my stories, and how I found my humanity by trying to bury it.

Put simply, I've been writing for as long as I can remember. One of my earliest memories is of sitting on my grandad's knee and telling him what to write while I drew the pictures, because I wasn't old enough to write words. I'd draw hundreds and hundreds of pictures of dinosaurs that all fit together into stories, embarrassing my mum by recreating situations I'd seen on nature documentaries.

When I was old enough to go to school, many of my early years were spent being bullied, excluded, and ignored. I knew back then that I was different, but I did not know why. Despite the great many children's books that ended with a moral of "be yourself," something about me was seemingly too different for people to accept. I hissed at people who hurt or scared me, and that only made things worse. Spitting like a llama worked briefly to stop people harassing me, but I was scolded for it worse than the people who hurt me.

It never really ended throughout my school years.

Throughout those years I found solace in books like *Watership Down* and *Warrior Cats*, where the characters were animals. Perhaps the theme of survival spoke to me; making it through my own days felt hard enough, so I could connect better to characters with such simple goals, where kinship felt simple and guaranteed. In time, this would lead to a vast collection of books, both modern and vintage, featuring creatures of all kinds, both real and mythical.

Far from gravitating towards high stakes, I preferred stories where the aim was simply to make it through the day. To find food. To make friends. To learn something new. I understood those needs and those problems. When animals were the central focus, interactions were less about subtle implications and unspoken rules, and more about the things that I knew and understood. Relationships developed organically, without the sort of drama that had me thinking, "Why don't you people just talk!"

When I ran out of books that I wanted to read, I started writing my own.

I started out writing about dragons flying through the air and breathing fire, and then moved on to cats. After getting pets that kept me company at home, I wrote about genetically engineered super-gerbils who had big pretty wings. I wrote three books about the Winged Gerbils, the main characters' names stolen directly from *Warrior Cats*. I wrote countless stories about characters who turned evil because of their own inner pains, becoming loners or getting lost in their own magical worlds.

Most of the time, though, I wrote about wolves. Bright colors and tragic backstories helped me live out fantasies where my characters were powerful, strong, not necessarily liked, but feared. Perhaps I thought that I just needed to be stronger or more intimidating, then the bullying would stop and the pain would go away. I wrote more than a few redemption arcs where these strong, sad characters made a single friend and finally felt loved. Someone being picked on for something they couldn't control and didn't understand was a common theme.

My favorite character (and possibly the most extravagant) was called Nahrell, a name that I made up myself. His tragic backstory was my favorite; he was a big grey wolf who was born with wings, which made the other wolves bully him. Nahrell's father ripped his wings off and gave him lots of scars, turning his fur bright red with blood. Eventually he became a necromancer who used his powers to bring countless plagues to the world of wolves.

I find Nahrell's story entertaining to reminisce on now, but as a 13-year-old I was extremely proud of it!

This time of my life ended when pride became embarrassment. This was a time when anything made by a teenage girl would be reviled and ridiculed, but it was also when browsing the internet yielded hundreds of guides about how to avoid making "bad" characters (also called "Mary Sues"). According to these guides, none of the characters I had made were "good."

After that, I stopped reading for a while in favor of video games. My favorite of all was *Okami*, where you played as a wolf-god with a paintbrush that shaped the world. I poured hundreds of hours into Sanctuary Woods' 1994 educational game *Wolf*, and its sequel, *Lion*. I combed hundreds of pages on different search engines looking for more. When they didn't exist, I studied a degree in game design to make them.

At age 19, I was diagnosed with autism. As I received the news, I felt a tangible relief. And then I started to laugh. It was as if the pieces had finally clicked into place.

Shortly before then, I had found a new special interest, which made a lot more sense knowing my diagnosis. The internet has always been a hub for small and isolated communities, and I found the places where writers ran wild and weirdness thrived. And for once, I thrived too.

Originating with war games in the 19th century, tabletop roleplaying games such as *Warhammer* and *Dungeons and Dragons* have been a staple of geek culture for decades. For those who don't already know, players take on the roles of fictional characters and go on grand, yet imaginary, adventures. The internet took that tradition, changed it, and made it something new, combining the mediums of writing and gaming to create something ever-changing, new, and unique.

I had discovered online RPGs.

My favorite was called *Origin*, a website which was conceived and designed by author Madison Trupp. I was originally drawn in because it combined almost everything that I loved. Animals, rocks and gemstones, bizarre fantasy worlds and uncovering mysteries from the dust. That was part of its charm, and part of its mystique.

Each character was born from nothing, and culture developed organically as more people added their own unique flairs. Groups formed rivalries or alliances, and lore developed as characters grew, aged, and died. Legends formed as characters discussed one another months or years later. Everything you could ever need was written down, somewhere. If you got lost, there was the guidebook!

My first character, a fox named Todd, was created on December 8, 2015. He was the simplest of my characters; just a baby fox who wanted to learn.

With thousands of animals available to play as, there were so many possibilities—and after Todd, I made so many characters! There was Kin-Kin, a wolf with a cape who many would have unaffectionately declared "a massive Mary Sue." A sad platypus named Destiny who was gradually dying as her magic gemstone slowly grew to pierce her brain. An angry otter (who was the counterpart to my husband's first character, a red panda). A weasel who literally turned green with envy, made a crown, and declared themself king.

Perhaps most importantly, I created one character who was a pile of goop in the shape of a dragon, whose story is perhaps the strangest of them all, and one of the few female characters I ever played. Years later, I can still describe her as a major part of my life. Remember how, from my early childhood, I dreamt of breathing fire and being able to fly? In one of these dreams I looked into a mirror and saw her there; an eldritch, inky dragon I named Nox.

Nox was kind, though sad; monstrous, yet oddly graceful and feminine. I dreamt of being her many times after that, whenever I felt particularly scared or particularly alone, but they were never nightmares.

I later came to realize that she was the perfect, unconscious expression of my dysphoria as a trans person.

On *Origin*, LGBTQ+ characters weren't anything unusual; in fact, they were the norm. So my characters became an outlet for feelings I couldn't possibly explain out loud. I had more than a dozen characters throughout my time on *Origin*, and more than half were male; others were genderfluid, genderless, or nonbinary. Only three were female: Destiny, Kin-Kin, and of course Nox. Through knowing them, I came to better know myself.

On the day I'm writing this, there are 19 male characters, 13 female characters, and 26 characters of other genders still active on the site. Some characters are nonbinary, agender, demiboys and demigirls, some genderfluid—and many, many more. Through *Origin*, I learned what all of those terms meant. Those identities were respected and normalized.

I came out as genderfluid, then trans, to my online friends before anyone else in my life knew. Far from being ridiculed or reviled, it was celebrated. I was offered congratulations without a hint of sarcasm. *Origin*'s players were my biggest supporters as I grew as a writer, and without them, I wouldn't be the author I am today. When we weren't crafting intricate and multi-layered stories, we were helping and supporting one another. And when we weren't doing that, we were discussing our lives, sharing recipes, or comparing the weather outside in different corners of the world.

By pretending to be a magical animal alongside a diverse array of other people, I found safety, and friends. Finally I was no longer alone.

I poured years of my life and hundreds of thousands of words into my *Origin* characters. I laughed, I cried, I lived out entire lives that weren't my own. I was shocked by the knowledge that there were people out there like me, with the same interests as me. And I had found them.

I began to realize that fantasy worlds make far more sense to me for a simple set of reasons. Science fiction and fantasy books which explore cultures that are different and new often need to explain even the most basic concepts of their worldbuilding and culture. Nothing can be assumed until it's written down. In general fiction, though, it is assumed that only the most niche or complex problems need to be explained. The author expects readers to have an implicit understanding of the world and its rules.

For me, and for many autistic people like me, that is too often not the case. The integral rules of socialization and society that people live by are never written down. There is no guidebook for life. We just have to drown in it until we learn to hide it.

Many people will tell you that the most integral rule of writing is show, don't tell. But I feel that this can be taken too far, rendering some forms of reading inaccessible. Many people like me struggle with what is left unsaid; sometimes we simply need to be told.

Origin, on the other hand, was a self-sustaining ecosystem full of talented artists, incredible writers, and amazing characters. I understood the unspoken rules, because I had watched them develop. People helped and taught each other if they found something hard to understand. I helped people too; after two years, I became a moderator, and then a Game Master. Unlike in the real world, I knew the rules here well enough to help run the game. By interacting with other people in the guise of magical animals, I had managed to make real, human friends. Because of those connections, those people, and those stories, it became easier to see myself as human, too.

Gradually, after five years of near-constant activity, I began to drift away from it all. Newcomers came, new characters were born, and old ones died. I began to lose track of the constantly developing story. On August 5, 2019, I posted a thread titled "This is Not an End," where I announced that I would be stepping back from my moderating and

Game Master duties, and closing up unfinished business by putting each of my characters into hibernation.

My last post was made on May 18, 2020.

I'm still friends with many of the wonderful people who were a part of my life during that time, many of whom still have characters that live and thrive to this day.

Before I left *Origin*, I started the first draft of a novel, the first I had written in five years. And, in an unbelievable stroke of character development, the main characters were human. As strange as it was writing about humans, I knew the story I wanted to tell could not be told any other way. It's a book about loneliness and isolation, which acknowledges that no matter how different or alone you may feel, you are never any less human. It was a message that I had once needed, but never seemed to find. In 2021, *Riftmaster* was released to the world.

Shortly after I finished my novel, I began to plan my wedding alongside my then-fiancée, Chris. We knew from the beginning that we wanted to create each other a gift of some sort. Something unique and wonderful that we could use to remember that day forever. So I fell back into a cozy cushion of nostalgia.

Our two favorite animals were the red panda and the river otter, and we had always loved to see them together. We had red panda and otter plushies, and we collected art depicting them together. Back in 2014 we had had this conversation in a noodle bar that has long since shut down:

"I was thinking last night," Chris said to me with a grin. "We should write a book together."

I looked up curiously from my pile of noodles. We'd tried to write a book together once before, and never finished it. I blinked, mouth full.

"You know how my favorite animals are red pandas, and yours are otters?"

"Yeah?"

"We should turn them into adorable aliens—red pandas and blue otters! From different planets, with different worlds. They'd start out thinking that they were so different, then the book would be all about them slowly becoming friends."

I grinned. "That would be cute. We should start it tonight! I'll write the otters, and you could write the pandas!"

We never finished that book. Chris brought his character from it into *Origin*, where he made a calm red panda as a counterpart to my feisty otter. The red panda and otter contrasted with the elements of fire and water was an idea we would return to time and time again.

After a while, Chris's red panda went back into hibernation, leaving my otter alone. But the story behind it was always a lingering thought in the back of my mind. And, three months before our wedding, I knew that it was time to bring that old spark of an idea back to life.

This time, rather than squirrelling away the animal characters I'd made, I brought them forward and nurtured them. To write about animals brought me warmth, comfort, and safety. I accepted this now, and I embraced it.

I went back to the people who had helped me find my place, who had made me who I am. The admins, who had produced beautiful and intricate artwork for the website, came to help. While I was writing, they worked together. They presented to me a book cover as a wedding gift from the entirety of *Origin*.

I brought back our characters, the otter and the red panda, and remade them, nurturing them, changing them both into something new.

On our wedding day, Chris gave me a beautiful, rainbow collage, filled with photos of us from throughout our years together. And I presented him with a book, *The Forge and the Flood*, which is about adorable aliens with very human problems. Befitting of a wedding, it's a story of unity, of joy, and of rainbows. Of two dramatically different families coming together. Hidden within it are the two characters that we made together, tiny snapshots of the lives we've shared and the people we've been.

Our wedding vows are framed with a tiny art piece: a blue otter and a red panda in the shape of a tiny heart.

The years have passed, the world has turned, and I'm a dramatically different person now than who I used to be. I know that I will always have a lot of people to thank for that. Somewhere along the line, I've taken on a little piece from all the characters I made, with the impulse of the otter and the energy of the weasel, and I unashamedly wear extravagance on my sleeve (whenever I get the chance, you'll find me wearing my signature cape!). I'm a mentor and a student, and to many an enigma. I'm not sure if my writing has influenced me, or whether those traits were there all along, just waiting for me to wake them up.

Even more than that, I have become the man I was always meant to be.

My characters still make odd cameos in my novels from time to time. I put them in there for my old friends to find and to smile at. The green weasel was one of them—if you read one of my novels, can you spot them?

One day, I'm hoping that Nox will be the star of her own book—an autobiographical children's book, which tells the story of my transition. My collection of books continues to grow to this day. I still love to write, to draw, to create. I know that a whole fantasy world's worth of people have my back. Because of the creatures I've known, and the people behind them, I'm autistic, proud, loud—but most of all, completely and unabashedly me. Every day, I'm bursting with excitement, because I know that there's so much more to come.

This has been a story of stories—one I hope is only the beginning!

I Like to Echo

Matrim Taitt

I like to echo. I have always liked to echo. I have a fascination with words, and sounds, and the way they feel as they leave my mouth, and so I say them. I say them a lot. Just as songbirds mimic the sounds of their fellows, producing clamoring calls removed from their original context for their own mysterious motivations, so do some people. Particularly autistic people.

I remember times when I was as a child, older than you might believe, singing a particular song lyric when I was in pain or in the midst of an anxiety attack. My mum knew by hearing that song that I, in some way, needed comfort, usually responding by singing back to me in kind.

It wasn't that I couldn't speak, it was that this song was the well-trod pathway that my stressed mind liked to travel. It was natural, though to strangers it was mindless babble.

Echolalia is what they call it; not solely an autistic trait, but one associated with us. It is a repetition of words and phrases as a form of communication, or as a soothing vocalization. An echolalic response might be to repeat a question back to the questioner in lieu of an answer, or perhaps to chant a beloved line previously delivered by your favorite TV character. As a child, that meant parroting phrases that meant nothing to the wider world but that could be parsed by family; as an adult, it means communicating mostly in memes. And honestly, privately, with close friends and with family, it still means to use those nonsense phrases to communicate those same feelings with those encoded meanings.

A recitation of a song lyric soothes the nerves when the world is too loud. A repetition of a word from the past with supportive associations is meant to communicate love in other connotations. "Imitation is the sincerest form of flattery" is, in my home, taken literally, when it comes to jokes that most would choose to simply appreciate.

(I know the whole quotation, but I am making the choice to stop half way, as it is not mediocre plagiarism but an unorthodox communication.)

It is a form of speech which I find comes naturally, and is full of freedom and glee when I'm speaking of things which excite me. Though, to follow, you have to know the key. If you can't understand my references then you might not see what I'm getting at.

Palilalia is similar to echolalia, but it is repeating one's own words instead of those taken from the mouths of others.

(Though where is the line between self and other? Tell me, are most turns of phrase not a configuration of words that are not our own invention?)

I can find myself reiterating an amusing word or phrase over, and over, and over again. An incessant chirping. It is often unconscious;

I don't realize I'm talking, or I haven't realized I've already explained something thrice or more because I get stuck in loops of speech, treading the same worn paths as before, unable to reach the listener. My tendency for redundancy forms a wall. I can sound like a broken record, but that is from your perspective. Your irritation forms a wall and my frustration cannot scale it. I don't know how to break through.

And then there's vocal stimming. Stimming is a contraction of the expression "self-stimulation," but that name did not catch on in the autistic community for reasons I'm sure you can imagine. It can take many forms: hand-flapping, foot-tapping, rocking, swaying, clicking, drumming. Absolutely anything that adds a sensory input to one in need of excitation. Stroking a scrap of fabric can drown out other unpleasant perceptions; fiddling with a pencil in a claustrophobic classroom can aid concentration; snapping fingers and clapping hands provides much-needed sensation—it feels good enough to do it again, and again, and again, and again. Stims can occupy any sense, including making noises. It's two for one, really: the sounds and the words are pleasant to hear, buzzing through the ear canal and causing delightful bursts of feeling, and the feeling of vibration through the throat and tongue and lips can soothe the itch that builds up through the day which needs to find some release.

I'm not an expert on these terms. I don't know where palilalia ends and echolalia begins. Is the repetition of a phrase which sets my nervous system ablaze a sign of echolalia or simple verbal stimming? Are they one and the same? A matter of purpose? Some websites say that the former is meaningless and the latter can be controlled, but if echoes can be used to communicate or emotionally regulate and I can go hours without realizing I've been chewing my tongue—literally chewing on my tongue, literally biting down as I think—then where does that leave that theory? And another query: what crosses the line from cultural approval—of singing a song or quoting a psalm—into neurodivergent oddity? Is it a matter of degree? The words which delight me? Google cannot tell me the difference between words of affirmation and self-stimulation. I think it foolish to dwell.

I do not know where palilalia ends and echolalia begins, but I can tell you which one I prefer to repeat.

All this is to paint you a picture of a child with a vocabulary borrowed from books a century old; a kid with an air of pretension, who used words too big for him with only a cursory understanding of their definition. And when those failed, a film quote might help smooth communication. A picture of an adult who built a script to navigate small talk; who answers the doorbell with an echoed chime; who hears a pleasing "bloop" in a video game and can't stop imitating the sound; who hears a question and echoes it back to buy some time to construct an answer.

But I haven't yet conveyed the absolute euphoria that comes from speaking words so perfect in their form that they have their own tactility. The way words like loquacious, like oubliette, like zenith or nadir, linger on my tongue like Armagnac, warming my palate with velvet multisyllabic undulations, while the fricatives and plosives spark my interest and pop in staccato prosecco bubbles. Words with wonderful vowel sounds wind around my tongue and rise up in my throat until they spill out in beeps and bloops that cause endless feedback loops; I hear the noise and echo it, stimulating my ears once more and repeating it. And when those words are sewn together into sentences, into paragraphs of lyrical prose that make me dance and sing, those are the moments I wouldn't change for anything. They make me happy that I cannot skim while reading. I linger on every word and soak up its meaning and intonation. I spend time with the text and learn the rhythms and intention.

These parroted phrases are not like the original. I do not have the skill to match the source; my accidental imitation of an accent is not skilled enough to make a profession from impressions. If I were at all musically talented, I might have found myself a songwriter. As it happens, I cannot string a set of notes together, so for a while my echoes were just for me. A soothing activity that made me smile, but nothing more.

And then, many years after life had shaken all enthusiasm from my bones, I came across a form of art that took a needle and thread to my heart and pulled it back together. It should not have been surprising to me but nevertheless was, you see, because I thought I hated poetry: from stuffy classroom lectures and dissected rhyming structures, to child-friendly subject matters. But, it turned out I hadn't looked in the right place.

It started with Poe and Yeats. I read them obsessively, read them aloud or, when necessary, silently for fear of annoying my housemates. I turned each word around inside my brain, rotated and examined them from every angle in my mind's eye and read them in a mental voice as vociferous and exultant as reality. And, later, I stumbled across verse that was more free. I found the Beat Generation, and jazz poetry. And on one cold night at 2 a.m. huddled under the blanket I allowed the YouTube algorithm to steer me towards spoken word, and I wept.

These were the loud and unselfconscious verses that held within them words so beautiful in complexity, or conversely in simplicity, that I could scarce believe they were real. In hearing this glorious chorus, I was awakened to a world in which my repetition in speaking was a feature, not a bug. These poets, though most presumably not autistic, nevertheless shared my inclination, my appreciation for patterns and alliteration. An echo could become a motif.

Despite my love for the medium, I am not an expert. I know the difference between an iamb and a trochee, but I still frequently get the two confused. Meter, and feet, and verse, all on their own merit beautiful words, are of less importance to knowing the poem than the sense contained within, at least for me. I find the rhythm and rhyme of the piece by listening, by parroting. Those clever poets crafting words that light my mind on fire and make my tongue tingle, that provide the innervation, innovation, that drives me, delights me—I could not admire them more.

It was interesting to learn that there was always a word for the harmony between vowels that I craved to hear and made quite clear the wonderous interconnected nature of the language I loved—that being "assonance." But, in all honesty, learning the word simply added a new stim to the repertoire; I already adored the concept of a repeated sound. It is the same with syncopation, though a much more satisfying word for sure: disruption of the flow was already something that made me feel euphoric in the tumbling fall of words from the lips of the artist. That anticipation transformed is a joy when performed, whether or not it can be defined.

And so, I devoured these poems with a fervor. It was at times an addiction, an unrelenting hunger. I found new phrases to mimic, new terms to adopt and assimilate, new songbirds to imitate. Some of these lines sank in so far that they etched themselves into my skin. Like a lyrebird, or perhaps given my proclivities a raven may be more appropriate, I quoted lines of scintillating verse that signaled my thirst for delicious, stimmy, sounds. My synesthesia knew no bounds. (And that word, synesthesia, how fun it is to say!)

Synesthesia: not solely an autistic trait but one associated with us. In my mind's eye words become sounds, which become textures and flavors. Some words are disgusting, and others ambrosia. I chewed upon the creations of those I think of as genius and reveled in the noise. The circuits in my brain that were once powered by the mundane were now fueled by art.

But how long before a lyrebird starts making its own music?

I started putting pen to paper, scratching words out across the page just as those same words walk through the deep grooves of my brain, those deep trenches where the sounds bounce in a cacophony of meaning. I was surprised, but very pleased, to find the lines came with lyrical ease. The poetry coalesced outside the framework of repetitive cadence to form the sentences almost effortlessly, breathlessly. I can display the sounds that make me feel alive in a way which gives them context, which allows them to shine around the dull light of auxiliaries and prepositions, and I can maybe make you fall in love with them too. Or, at least, that's what I aim to do.

I was never fond of rules. I railed against the confines of linguistic tradition in favor of more unusual forms of writing; I know it's not great to switch up tenses too often in a single passage but what else can I do when some ideas just sound better in present? And punctuation marks? Those rules are more a guideline; I subscribe to the notion that they are there to spell the motion of the words. They are not prescriptive, they are simply descriptive of breaths, of pauses. To be still a moment and bathe in the emotion evoked in the passages.

Writing more poetically allowed me to be free of the chill haze that clung to prose that was too afraid to be purple. The rhythms of my speech drove the hypnotizing beat of my fingertips on the keyboard. Words which failed to come while attempting non-fiction instead spilled from my mind in a fountain of feeling. I am never more happy than when I'm creating.

I spend hours agonizing over a verse or a title, to edit the style, just so, until perfect. That's hyperfixation; again, not solely an autistic trait but one associated with us. The words consume me, the chaotic and unforgiving world blocked out behind the pages I have written. I am in a paper-wrapped world of my own creation and I exist there in absolute equilibrium, content to remain in that nest for eternity. But, when I emerge, when I try to make the writing easy for others to follow, I get lost in which parts to cut. It loses the musicality, and not in a way that is interesting. The divergence from the beat feels messy and unintentional. Not exactly palatable. The flow is lost amid my efforts to sound more profound, or to tighten it up into something that's snappy. There is a value in brevity. And I'm not very witty. It loses all rhythm, but that's alright; I'll dial it in. Perhaps one day I'll be brave enough to stand behind the microphone.

I have so many poems, poems that will never see the red pen of an editor, will never even see another set of eyes linger upon them. They exist for my pleasure alone. And that's where the second half of that proverbial phrase attributed to Wilde comes into acute focus: "Imitation is the sincerest form of flattery that mediocrity can pay to greatness." Because as a poet I am...clumsy. And that's okay. The rhymes may be trite, the meter unparsable, but that doesn't matter in the slightest. The joy is in the creation, the imagination, the recitation. The self-indulgence is the point. It's stimming, brimming with elation.

If I can string together a sequence of sounds to stimulate my senses with syllables of similarity then I'm satisfied, whether or not it's enjoyable to a neurotypical audience. If I can speak my lines to the beat of a drum, thrumming with rhythm and flush with aplomb, echoing the cadence but not quite a song, then who cares about the technicalities? If chirruping the same words again and again in neurodivergent echoes makes me feel as free as the soaring birds I resemble, then what does it matter that the simile is stretched and slightly pretentious? The fun is in the wordplay, in the expression. I like words. I like saying them. I like saying them a lot.

My brain is hard-wired to play around with sounds, to mimic tones, to hyperfixate on the noises you make, to find poetry hidden in prose. I cannot help but celebrate the reason my mind works this way, because I was asked to write an essay, and instead, I've given you this. I have enjoyed every second of creation; it's been an autistic celebration. So yes, I like—I love—to echo.

All Cats Are Autistic

Laura Kate Dale

When I say the phrase "all cats are autistic," I do not in any way mean that in a literal sense. I am not a psychologist, or a veterinarian, or some kind of hybrid profession specializing in the diagnosis of human mental health conditions in broad categories of animals.

I am not, literally, diagnosing all cats on planet Earth as autistic.

However, in a more personal and figurative sense, I have always seen a lot of myself as an autistic person in my relationship with cats, and our shared needs, temperaments, and behaviors.

I am autistic, and when I find interacting with human beings complicated, confusing, and hard to navigate, I find that cats offer a reassuring counterbalance in my life. I may not be able to read non-verbal body language and unspoken subtext in humans, but I often can in cats, because so much of the way they communicate feels like it's part of a language that they share with autistic humans.

Ever since I was a young child, I have been the kind of person who prefers cats over dogs as a social companion. No judgment to people who prefer dogs—find your joy and companionship where you can—but for me dogs were everything I struggled to handle, when it came to both people and pets.

Dogs were loud, energetic, overexcitable, and extremely socially extroverted. I know this is a blanket statement, and many of you out there with dogs will insist your dogs are nothing like this, but throughout my life this has been my personal experience. I am not here to convince you not to like dogs, or to have you convince me I have just not met the right dog. Dogs, as a broad category, do not mesh well with me, and my experience of the world.

Dogs are that person at a social gathering who is determined to talk to you, whether you want them to or not. They're the person who insists you get up and dance, despite not being comfortable doing so, because you looked like you were sitting alone not having fun, discounting that your version of fun might simply be more quiet and isolated than theirs.

Dogs are that person with an unlimited social battery, energized by being around people, excited and exaggerated, no matter the situation. They're the people who find quiet and calm deathly boring, and who need something to be constantly happening that they can be taking part in. Every moment needs to be filled with activity. If you just want to sit quietly, in their presence but not necessarily interacting directly very much, they assume something is wrong, and that you're either lacking encouragement to do something, or upset in some way you're not explaining, rather than simply at ease with quiet coexistence.

Dogs are, to me, the physical manifestation of direct, constant, sustained social interaction. They're also a sensory nightmare, with no sense of respect for physical space. They want to be your best friend right this second, in physical contact with you, begging for your attention. If touch is not your love language, tough luck, they're going to greet you with physical contact when you get home, because they're just so excited to see you.

I hope you're okay with big forceful hugs, and kisses all over your face without warning.

That was never right for me.

I went undiagnosed on the autism spectrum until my late teen years, but all throughout my childhood the signs that I was autistic were there: the rigid hyperfixations, the strict adherence to rules and structure, the sensory struggles, the stimming behaviors, and the difficulties socializing with my non-autistic peers.

Growing up, I was very much a child who engaged in solo play. I would sit in my childhood bedroom organizing trading cards and action figures, lining them up in formation, putting them away, then laying them back out in formation.

I wasn't seeking out group social interactions.

I did, however, find emotional connection in our first pet cat, who I am going to name Skittles in this essay, because the name of your first pet is a depressingly risky piece of information to publish in our modern world.

Skittles was a small, slender, plain black cat. She was quiet, skittish, and enjoyed quiet cuddles on her own terms.

It wasn't that she didn't like cuddles; she would often curl up on a family member's lap and fall asleep for an evening, actively purring with joy for the warmth and connection. The thing with Skittles was that she liked physical contact, but initiated on her own terms. You had to let her come to you, not make a big deal of the situation, be gentle and not too forceful with your interactions, and give her space to leave when she was ready.

Skittles, like most cats in my life, was prone to overstimulation. If there was too much noise coming from the vacuum cleaner, or too many new people she didn't know in the house, or someone was being too persistent in trying to pet her, she would get visibly distressed, and in extreme cases lightly lash out. Lashing out at people was never her first choice—she would always try first to get up and walk away, finding somewhere quiet away from the sensory sensation that was causing her discomfort, but would lash out if put in a position where she had no other way of getting away from what was distressing her.

Skittles loved being around people, but on her own terms. It wasn't that she didn't like people, she just found new ones overwhelming.

As long as you gave Skittles space to come to you when she wanted to socialize, followed her lead when she told you with a look she didn't want any more petting, and let her set the terms on which she socialized, she was a sweet, soft, cuddly baby who loved being around people.

Skittles had a routine, one she stuck to religiously; from waking up at a set time expecting to be fed, through to wanting company standing nearby when she ate, she had a way she lived life, and she stuck to it.

Now, I know I am generalizing again here. All cats have wildly different personalities, but in my experience, much of the above is true of most cats, to a greater or lesser degree. I think that's why, ever since childhood, I have felt a unique kinship toward the cats in my life as an autistic person.

I love physical contact, it's something I emotionally crave, but I need to be able to initiate it, on my own terms, and step away from that contact when it becomes too much for me. I get overwhelmed by loud sensory situations and crowds of new people, and always prefer to remove myself from a situation I know is going to cause me distress, rather than be forced to stay in that situation and let that discomfort build to a point where it's overwhelming. I stick to a predictable routine, feeling stressed and anxious when it changes too much.

I feel like I've always seen a lot of myself in cats, and a lot of them in me. We both need sensory contact on strict terms, require time alone, dislike changes in routine, and appreciate a gentle and calm approach to interaction.

As an adult with a formal autism diagnosis, it's pretty easy for me to look back and dissect why I felt this connection to cats growing up. However, as a child experiencing that connection, it was a lot less about understanding that these parallels existed, and a lot more about seeking connection I was failing to find in the humans in my life.

Like many autistic people, I got bullied by my peers growing up for being nebulously, unquantifiably "weird." It's easy to pick on the kid who has really obvious triggers that lead to them being distressed, and it's easy to do things that wouldn't distress anyone else, and get away with it as benign behavior rather than targeted bullying of someone with a disability.

I also found people in my family difficult to connect with, as all too often it felt like they and I were speaking incompatible languages. I didn't have a vocabulary to explain why social situations, multi-textured foods, and changes in routine were so stressful and upsetting, which made it difficult to establish boundaries around my needs, or explain that needing time alone, away from the family, was not a sign that I disliked them as people.

My first cat, Skittles, was probably my first proper friend growing up. I would verbally confide in her when times were tough. I would seek her comfort when I felt sad, and I relied on her to feel less alone.

In a world where all too often, my being autistic drove away people in my life who I desperately sought understanding and connection from, Skittles was there, communicating in a language that made sense to me. I never had to explain to her that sitting in silence near her, not talking, didn't mean I was secretly mad at her. I never had to justify the activities I was finding joy in, or why I was repetitively moving my body in ways others did not. She was company, without constant demands that I perform interaction and sociability in some rigidly defined way.

I'm now in my early 30s, and I don't see myself ever living a life where I don't own a cat. I currently live with Smudge, a cat my family owned as Skittles was getting older. When my parents moved away from the country for a few months, on a winter retreat a few years ago, they asked me if I'd like to take Smudge on as my own, and she's lived with me ever since.

Smudge is a calico, and she loves physical contact on her own terms. She likes to be a scarf, up around the necks of people she knows, laid across their shoulders, up at face level. She loves attention and physical contact, but only on her own terms. She gets overwhelmed by loud sounds, like the vacuum cleaner, and struggles with changes in setting and routine.

Smudge is not, in a diagnosable sense, autistic. But, as far as being a social companion I can feel safe and understood around, she'll always be autistic to me.

If you've ever been unsure how to emotionally connect with an autistic person in your life, if you treat them the way you would a cat, you're probably 99 percent of the way there.

Curtain Call

Sarah Lloyd-Slifkin

Whenever I hear the term "masking," my mind travels to the stages of ancient Greece, where actors donned masks as they performed incredible plays that still make up the backbone of theater today. My mind also goes to the autistic definition of "masking," seeing as how many autistic people acquaint themselves with their own style of performance in their everyday life.

We learn to speak and gesture and react to the world around us in a way an allistic person would, and how to walk among neurotypicals by consciously mirroring their every move, and use that knowledge to navigate a neurotypical world that isn't always kind to us as a means of survival. But while the Greeks delivered beautiful speeches and epic tales of gods wreaking havoc on traumatized mortals, those of us who mask our autism make ourselves invisible. Even if the process isn't as fun as performing a monologue by Euripides, the average autistic person becomes more skilled in the art of acting than anyone would expect, even if that reality still isn't reflected in the theater industry itself.

I still can't decide if acting is the most or least autistic-friendly field of all time.

On the one hand, acting is an endeavor that's contingent on everyone involved following an endless stream of rules. Ever since I took it up as a childhood hobby, I loved the structure that came with doing theater. I loved taking direction on everything I did, and the sensation of someone explaining to me exactly how I needed to do something as simple as walking in a circle or taking a breath. I loved poring over lines for hours at a time, and the accompanying sensation that comes with always knowing what to say, even if I stumbled over my words in front of people when I was offstage. Most of all, I loved working for months on end until I was at a point where I knew everything that would happen—what I would say, and wear, and do—for the next few hours of my life, and repeating that same sequence for nights at a time. After all, when you clap your hands or repeat something over and over, it's a stim. But when a character does it, it's nothing more than character work.

On the other hand, an under-acknowledged side of acting is how much the most successful performances begin offstage. While acknowledging it directly is taboo, a huge portion of landing a role has to do with whether or not someone on the creative team likes you.

Of course, this isn't to say that personal connections and talent are mutually exclusive! Plenty of directors gravitate towards someone they've worked with in the past because they understand firsthand how well an actor can bring a character to life, or in the hopes of creating as stress-free a creative experience as possible. That said, this approach makes it difficult for new actors to get their foot in the door, and it especially complicates finding opportunities for people who struggle with social intelligence.

While anyone who's met actors can stereotype them as wildly extroverted and quick to make a great first impression, actors who skimp on the networking and schmoozing that goes into getting a role are always going to be at a disadvantage, and that might have something to do with the reason why autistic people are still a minority in the world of theater.

In almost 20 years of honing my craft as an actor, I learned very quickly not to come across as "too autistic" around other theater people. This was especially true of directors, who had the final say over what role I'd be playing in a production. And, as loath as theater people who don't struggle with social interactions are to admit it, the impressions that actors and other theatermakers leave on directors and producers play a key part in determining whether or not they're given an opportunity to work on a production.

As you might imagine, this bias creates obstacles for all sorts of neuroatypical people, and as an autistic aspiring actress, I was no exception.

Over time, I'd gotten pretty skilled at anticipating how difficult a production would be before even stepping in for an audition. The most comfortable auditions I'd ever experienced all made the audition material as accessible as possible; I could find online exactly what song and scene the casting team expected me to perform weeks in advance of the audition date, with fully detailed character descriptions and other supplementary material (e.g. links to past performances or deeper production information) that informed me of how to develop my approach ahead of time.

Thorough breakdowns of the audition process were rare, but did wonders for putting me at ease before showing up. That foresight is especially crucial to autistic people, when we're already anxious about maneuvering through a new social situation and presenting ourselves to groups of people for approval.

Every one of my worst auditions had a lack of that careful forewarning in common. One director had the distinct privilege of leaving me with three of my worst-ever audition experiences across a span of about four years. I'd show up to auditions of his, thinking I was entirely prepared, only to be shouted at in front of other aspiring cast members for doing a warm-up exercise incorrectly, or to earn his deep annoyance when I didn't walk into the casting room having memorized material he never made public for actors. Another time, I showed up ready to sing for a musical theater audition, but only found out after walking in the audition room that I'd be singing with a CD instead of with an accompanying pianist or a cappella. When he hit play, the track was in a completely different key from the sheet music we'd practiced with, without any cue in the music for when to start singing, leaving me hopelessly off-tempo and out of tune in a song I'd previously been confident about performing.

That disaster prompted me to break the unspoken rule of auditions, which is to never stop mid-performance and ask for a redo—which has always been another kick to my own brand of autistic perfectionism. He obliged, with irritation on his face that even I could read, but I choked down tears and heard myself fail again to keep in time with the music. I left the room so rattled that I slipped out of my allistic actor's mask and left the room with a curt thanks, avoiding eye contact with anyone else until I could make my way home and cry.

It wasn't until I went to college that I found an acting mentor who left me feeling at ease even as I tried to relax the pressure I put on myself to mask my autism around allistic people. Ellen was a professor of acting and directing, and it didn't take me long to see that she was totally comfortable with herself and every one of her students in all of our eccentric glory. All of the facets of my autistic self that made me stick out in a room full of fellow theater nerds—my hesitation to jump into bubbly conversations with other actors, or my quiet focus on whatever material I'd prepared for the week—made me a promising, dedicated student in her eyes. That was probably why, two years into working with me, she approached me with the offer to be her assistant director for an upcoming college production of *The Curious Incident of the Dog in the Night-Time*. Hearing the name of one of the only plays centering an autistic character's perspective, I blurted out the fact that I'd be thrilled to work on it, as an autistic person.

"You're autistic?" she asked with a stunned expression.

Before I could let the fear of damaging our professional relationship dissuade me from accepting her offer, a grin spread across her face. "That's great!" Her genuine glee wiped away all of my momentary panic, and the ambitious plans she quickly laid out afterwards about recruiting autistic performers and consultants to make the show a respectful representation of my community left me feeling hopeful.

For the first time, a professional asked me that day to contribute my perspective, in all its autistic glory, in making something special. It was something I hadn't thought possible up to that point, and as time went on, I was touched again and again by what it looked like to see autistic talents uplifted.

Ellen stuck to her commitment to honor the autistic community, re-searching autistic artists to inform our production design and making clear from preliminary design meetings onward that she wouldn't stand for sound or set design that could overwhelm the senses of autistic audience members. She partnered with our campus Disabled Student Alliance, consulting with autistic student advocates and inviting them to production meetings to offer their input. And, before auditions even began, she offered one autistic alliance member she hit it off with the play's leading role—a delicious inversion of the ableist offstage favoritism I laid out earlier if there ever was one—and made a point at auditions of discreetly allowing actors to volunteer whether or not they were autistic.

As I found myself on both sides of the casting table for once, I was thrilled to note that about a third of our cast was, in fact, openly autistic—including myself, in a small role.

This was my first time operating as both an actor and a member of a production's creative team, and the experience opened up a new concept of what theater could be. Whenever I wasn't rehearsing as an actor, I'd be taking notes for Ellen or supervising the rest of the cast, chiming in as we figured out blocking (basically, what we needed the actors to do onstage). This last dimension proved incredibly important, as our production was easily the most high-concept play I'd ever taken part in.

The Curious Incident of the Dog in the Night-Time centers on the journey of a young autistic boy named Christopher as he navigates a series of mysteries, and goes on an adventure that takes him far outside of his comfort zone. While the play itself assumes its audience consists mostly of allistic people, it relies on both Christopher's long stretches of dialogue explaining his thought processes, and scenes artistically depicting common autistic experiences like literal-minded interpretation or sensory overload. Our production relied on a group of actors playing multiple parts across the play's runtime, and spending time when we weren't playing a character giving voice to Christopher's inner thoughts and feelings, making us a physical manifestation of his inner world across the story.

I most vividly remember a climactic scene where Christopher, discovering a shocking truth about his family, breaks down from the sheer force of his upset. Tasked with embodying the crescendo of feelings that go into a meltdown, our team worked with a professional movement coordinator and shared ideas about the scene, settling on using common stimming gestures as a starting point, before our movements would shift into something increasingly desperate as control gets away from Christopher.

Here, for the first time, I would stim onstage, and it wouldn't be as a joke or a character tic, but as a representation of a coping mechanism—as a representation of one of the reasons I stim in my everyday life.

Sitting at the start of this immensely powerful scene, and listening to the feelings of helplessness and fear that Christopher experiences, I let myself react to his situation as I would in real life—fingering my clothes, flapping my hands, covering my ears, or whatever else struck me in the moment—and got nothing but praise for channeling the spirit of the scene around me with my whole heart. For the first time, I was embodying a moment onstage without having to filter it through the lens of what a "normal" reaction would be. I was finally reacting organically, without coaxing myself into acting—what every book, director, and theater class called on me to do. I only needed the opportunity to do it.

That moment of watching everyone around me rise to the challenge of respecting autism with dignity stood as a challenge to every petty excuse I'd ever heard about the struggle to put autism onstage. I'd seen plenty of productions with common autistic traits—gesticulation, echolalia, literal-mindedness, and more—deployed as a punchline or a shorthand for strangeness. I couldn't help but ask myself: if anyone on the team of those productions, be they director, playwright, or actor, had been autistic, would I have seen autism celebrated onstage sooner? And, if I had, would it still feel like the end of the world whenever my mask started to slip off in front of the people around me? Or would all of my anxieties about my autism feel just a little bit less heavy?

Production meetings gave way to rehearsals, and rehearsals ended in time for performances. As with any other show, I had my own share of mixed-up lines and little missteps across our shows, but the different response from the cast and crew left me with an entirely new sensation, a feeling of support.

In the past, tripping on my way offstage or delivering dialogue from the wrong part of the script left me queasy at the idea that it reflected on my failings as an actor. Navigating the unspoken rules of social interaction and masking in front of directors and actors overwhelmed me to the point that any little error I made onstage felt like it would cost me a world of future opportunities. This time, though, I knew my mistakes wouldn't challenge the trust Ellen and the rest of our team had in me; I felt the understanding everyone had for me across the entire time we spent working on the play.

Instead, if I felt any disappointment in myself, it was only because I put so much of myself into our show that I wanted it to be the best it could possibly be. And, as scary as that experience could be, it was a huge step forward in my development, and a relief from all of the pressure and angst I'd worked myself into over years of working in theater.

Partway through our run, Ellen arranged a talkback segment after one of our shows. Here, the entire cast would field questions from the audience about our experience with the show, with an emphasis on our openly autistic cast members discussing how they felt throughout the creative process. Emceed by one of the leaders of the Disabled Student Alliance, it would let us discuss theater from a proudly autistic point of view. This would be the first time I'd be standing in front of a crowd of people I didn't know and acknowledging myself as part of the autistic community, and I knew that, for most of the people in the audience, what we said could be their first time listening to autistic people talking about their experiences on their own terms.

I wrung my hands over the question of how I should participate, for reasons both logically flimsy ("Who am I to talk over people who've been living their entire lives as proud of their autism, when I've spent so much time denying this part of myself?") and downright ignorant ("What right do I have to qualify myself as 'autistic enough' to speak?" and "How would embracing my autism in public affect my future as an actor, if anyone else from the theater department sits in on the talk?"). Ultimately, I resolved to participate, but without taking up any more time than I needed to.

When I finally walked onstage though, leaving my character and my directing responsibilities at the door, all of my hang-ups fell away. As the cast was asked to stand if they identified as autistic, I stood tall and proud in a way I never had before, secure in the lineup of other members of my community as we let the audience cheer us on. Listening to my fellow cast members' voices, I wasn't grabbing for my next line or feverishly running through blocking, but letting myself focus entirely on each word as they shared their experiences. The confidence they projected surrounding their identity bowled me over, as they shared stories of receiving diagnoses at young ages, or joining networks dedicated to supporting our shared identity.

When it was finally my turn to share, I surprised myself by bringing up Christopher's arc and the way it differed from my own life story. Thinking through what I would say, I let the audience listen to the thoughts I'd kept inside of me for years as I elaborated what I'd experienced as an autistic woman, and as a person with autism who'd taken great pains to hide such a key part of myself from the people around me. I shared anecdotes about people I'd cared for betraying my trust and revealing their own hidden bigotries, and the moments where theater felt like a survival tool or an escape from ableism altogether.

As I spoke, I understood what it meant to be onstage without an inner voice telling you what to do, and how it felt to have an audience enraptured not by the expectation of a theatrical show, but by me, on my own terms.

Speaking to that audience, unsure of what I would say next, was the most present I have ever been on a stage, even after hours dedicated to the craft of operating in the moment as an actor.

The show eventually came to a close and the end was, as you'd expect, even more bittersweet than any other piece of theater I'd ever done.

Saying goodbye to the rest of our creative team brought with it its own set of revelations: one cast member told me that my answers at the talkback were so moving that her mom cried; our alliance-recruited lead actress was considering getting more involved in the theater scene on campus; and our movement coordinator confided in me that working on the show made her start seriously considering the possibility that she could be autistic.

That last insight still brings me to happy tears whenever I think about it, because how often can someone say that their time on a play left them re-examining their sense of self in such a meaningful way?

The Curious Incident of the Dog in the Night-Time left me with a journey of self-reflection ahead of me, too. For as long as I could remember, I'd thought of acting as my identity, and as my future. I'd dedicated upwards of a decade to becoming as good at performing as I could possibly be, even when it cost me tremendously in terms of my self-esteem and well-being, because the end results always left me fulfilled. But, now that I'd seen exactly what theater could do for me—the enthusiasm and kindness Ellen greeted me with as her protege, the thrill of telling a story that resonated deeply with me and seeing how it affected others, and, most of all, the breathless happiness of sharing all of myself at that talkback without punishment hanging over my head—I didn't know how I could ever go back.

I kept on with my theatrical studies, and joined in on a few more productions before earning my degree, but something permanently shifted in how I understood theater. For too long, I'd practiced loving theater as best as I could in the hopes that it would compensate for my autism. Now, I asked myself if theater would love my autistic self back.

Since that magical experience ended, I've finally made my way to a place where I don't define myself by how well I wear a mask. Without staking my happiness on the approval of an imaginary director, I've made a promise to myself that, wherever my passions may take me, it'll be somewhere that enables more moments of autistic joy.

Without Shame

Jane Magnet-Dale

On Wednesday August 10, 2021, I was joined by some of my dearest friends to celebrate my wedding day.

Laura and I are both autistic, and while it may be something of a stereotype for autistic people to be really into trains, it's hard to express the excitement we shared having the privilege of getting married on one.

I've been to a good number of weddings for other people, and one thing I have always struggled with is formal wear. It's always smart, but uncomfortable or restrictive in ways that drive me to distraction.

For our day, we stated there would be no formal dress code. Dress as fancy or as casual as you like, and that went for us brides too. While Laura wanted a big, fancy white dress, I wore a multicolored tie dye dress in a very soft fabric which I'd removed the labels from. Instead of the court shoes I'd usually wear to such an event, I was in a fresh pair of comfortable, canvas high-tops.

Our wedding bouquets were beautifully made for us from fabric, meaning that I didn't have to deal with the sensory confusion of holding real flowers for the whole day. I did my own makeup, I didn't need any help getting into my dress, and while it was multilayered, I didn't have to get assistance from anyone to use the bathroom at any point.

Consequently, while I was surrounded by a lot more people than I'm usually comfortable with, and wearing unfamiliar clothes, I was only a little overwhelmed by the love and attention, as opposed to uncomfortable textures and sensations. It was a day of love, laughter, bad puns, happy stimming, and dancing in the aisles of a train traveling at up to 125 mph out of London Euston.

Looking through the photo album afterwards I see page after page of smiling faces, including my own, genuine, smile.

After being told for years that I needed to smile more, or do it "better," I taught myself a practiced "acceptable" smile using a WikiHow article. I've been told it's "a beautiful smile," "so genuine," and how "it lights up your whole face." The thing is, I can always tell the difference between that performative smile, done for the benefit of others, and that which comes naturally when I feel it. What I see in those wedding photographs is the real and genuine article, because on that day I didn't have to perform for anyone. My comfort needs were accounted for, and I was with someone who makes me feel safe to be exactly who I am and how I am.

As a child I was told off for many things, often without comprehending why such things were forbidden. When I asked questions to try and gain such understanding, I was—rather unhelpfully—told off for that too. One of my most prolific offences was the making of noise. In our house there was to be no whistling, humming, singing (unless you're really good at it, which I was assured I was not), no clicking of tongues, no sighs above a certain volume, no attempted beatboxing, and no generally weird mouth sounds.

The problem was that a line from a show, or section of a song, would get stuck in my brain. Then, without even thinking about it, I might just start repeating it aloud.

As an adult who has taken time to understand my autism, I know this is an example of echolalia (the unsolicited repetition of vocalizations made by others). Like most of my so-called quirks growing up, it was just something I felt compelled to do, and I lacked the language or self-awareness to explain that to my elders. When my parents demanded to know why I did these things, I'd usually fall quiet, stare at the ground, and mutter, "I don't know." This was usually countered with a demand that I look at them when I'm talking, and to speak up.

Another way I irritated my parents was by "fidgeting." They strongly desired stillness, where I was compelled to stim, to move. When bouncing up and down on my toes was forbidden, I started flapping my arms. When that was too much, I started clicking my fingers. When that was punished, I moved to clapping my fingers against my palms. When that was too noisy, I picked up something I'd seen on television: I started doing piano finger exercises, tapping each finger against my thumb in order, up and down from pinky to index and back. It was quiet and subtle enough to usually go unnoticed. On occasion though, even that was too much and I would be forced to sit on my hands.

Whenever I started getting into something (a TV show, a toy, a science subject, etc.) I just wanted to talk about it all the time. I wanted to share the thing that was bringing me joy, and hopefully see something reflected back at me from my audience. Unfortunately, family and school peers alike wanted none of it. What they wanted from me was simply my silence and/or absence.

Once I realized that no one else cared about the things that excited me I stopped trying to share my interests with other humans. Eventually I bought myself a Commodore 64, using my saved Christmas, birthday, and secretly unspent lunch money. One of my fondest memories of that machine was using the manual to teach myself how to code, and then writing a program I could have conversations with. My coding wasn't very clean, but thanks to those thousand or so lines of code, I could regularly and at length interact with something that never complained about the experience. I made a friend.

The one thing I found that proved acceptable to share was jokes. When I got them (and I often didn't), I loved jokes. When I didn't get them, but observed that other people did, and had enjoyed them, I did my best to remember them.

Unfortunately, I faced three major problems:

1. My memory wasn't great.

2. Due to sensory processing issues, I often misheard things, meaning that even when I thought I was telling them correctly, I really wasn't.

3. For the most part, you can only tell each joke to a person once. Repeat tellings are discouraged.

My only hope was to analyze the jokes which I was sure I had understood, and to try and write my own. What I clumsily came to understand was that thanks to the English language being kind of a mess, many words have more than one definition, and plenty of others sound similar to one another.

Yep, I discovered puns. I was in love with puns.

Other people, however, do not love puns. Countless times throughout my life I've heard puns described as the lowest form of humor. Once again, I had a thing that brought me little portions of joy, but for reasons I couldn't understand I had to keep it to myself or face the pun-ishment (I will not apologize).

There are plenty of reports about how neurodiverse people, diagnosed or not, can end up with symptoms of complex post-traumatic stress disorder. This comes as a result of having survived to adulthood in a world that often doesn't understand us and that we can find incredibly overwhelming. At the same time, we're frequently forced to appear sufficiently neurotypical in order to be accepted by peers and seniors alike.

Once I left home I spent a lot of time in flat shares. Keeping to my own room meant that my stims, tics, and other quirks could be privately expressed to some degree. That said, I held a lot inside even in private, partly due to fear of being discovered, and partly from the shame I'd been taught in my youth.

Living with romantic partners was a very different matter, however. If I wanted to go and lie in a dark room to decompress, it was often seen as wanting to get away from them. If I was really enjoying a piece of music and wanted to listen to it on repeat for hours at a time, I was being annoying. If I wanted to sit quietly and do my own thing while they watched TV, I was being antisocial. If I felt the urge to go for a three-hour walk, after midnight, on my own, I was being suspicious, and likely sleeping around, after which there would be demands to see my phone every few hours to check who I was talking to.

When it came to decorating our homes, partners would fill our spaces with scented candles which must never be lit, photographs of their family, random bowls of colorful beads, and unusual objets d'art. My collections of video game memorabilia, and various types of puzzles, were to be hidden away in a cupboard. The things I took joy from being surrounded by were always "mess" or "junk" and not the sort of things adults should be seen to have just lying around the house.

Inevitably (or so I thought), at some point in a relationship, my partner and I would end up in heated arguments. Almost without fail there would come a time when I would start to stutter. My words caught behind my front teeth and looped or sputtered to a complete halt.

I find my stutter extremely frustrating. It only manifests when I'm extremely distressed, and usually when I most need to explain myself. Unfortunately, fighting against it is completely fruitless and always ends with a complete shutdown. Voice.exe has encountered a fatal exception and must be closed.

Meanwhile my partner would be glaring or screaming at me for failing to respond or answer questions. In a desperate struggle to communicate I would attempt crude sign language or offer to text my responses. Signs were taken as silent treatment, and texting was soundly rejected as discourteous.

When one of us finally did just walk away, I would try to explain myself via text anyway. Inevitably, this was taken as cowardice. Many refused to read my messages: they'd just come to confront me, saying, "If you've got something to say, say it to my face."

Some partners took even the smallest or most involuntary actions as cause for extreme annoyance at the embarrassment that I caused them. When I tried to tap my fingers as a way to get through dinner with their parents, I was being distracting. When I put my hands under the table to hide that I was doing so, I was told it looked like I was playing with myself. When an anxious tic caused me to loudly meow during dessert you'd have thought I'd started finger painting crude pornography with chocolate sauce on their fancy tablecloth, given the reaction it caused.

That all changed when I first started dating Laura. Unlike a lot of past relationships, I felt like I knew her pretty well, having listened to a couple of video game podcasts she hosted. That had allowed me a good idea of her sense of humor, and the confidence that should I throw out a good-bad pun or two, it wasn't going to be a deal-breaker for her.

A lot of our early time together was spent just making each other laugh, with marathon pun sessions going on for most of a day, and sometimes, into the next. A quiet moment was often greeted with a gleeful "You're trying to think of another one, aren't you?" We'd slip into various voices and characters and play out the most ridiculous scenes with barely a drop of shame. In the moments where doubt did creep in, we were quick to reassure each other. "Never stop, I love your jokes, even and especially when they're awful."

The ability to so openly love a thing, and to share it with another person, was amazing and extremely liberating. It wasn't just jokes though; we talked about all sorts of things, at extreme length. Now, you may say that that's just a typical new relationship thing, getting to know each other, but it was so much more than that.

There were so many times where we would allow ourselves to get completely carried away, infodumping about trains, music, Lego®, the history of board games, and more at length. At first this was regularly punctuated with apologies for "going on for so long." Each time we reassured the other that it was more than okay to do so, and each time we trusted ourselves to go a little longer.

Having listened to Laura talk in detail about her interests and deriving great joy from the exuberance that crept into her as she did so, I thought about the people who'd taught me not to express myself in that way. I honestly don't understand how someone can encounter a person who gleefully wants to share their greatest interests and doesn't get at least a little caught up in their excited energy.

Laura was the first adult I met who had a diagnosis of autism (though I know several people who have extremely strong suspicions that they are autistic but don't feel the need to seek a formal diagnosis). Consequently, when we did finally meet, I wanted to ask her about what sort of things she might need from me (or specifically not need) if she was experiencing sensory overload or meltdown.

In having that conversation, I thought more about my own needs: how I also sometimes needed a quiet space, or not to be touched when I'm distressed (so many people will try to hug a person in distress, and it can be extremely counterproductive), or to not have my movements commented on. As a result, I started to feel safe to ask for those things for myself. I can't really express how much effort that took to finally do so, and then how much again it took to actually lower my defenses to engage with my needs around Laura. I had to break a lifetime of conditioning, but I did eventually get there.

Laura has never forbidden me from making sounds (sometimes, she needs some silence for focus or sensory input regulation, but that's separate). She's never told me off for beatboxing, and she's never complained about the fact that I regularly sing most of the first line of a particular song but never get any further. She's never scolded me for putting on a voice and talking back and forth with our cat at length about hypothetical cat parties she has with all her friends when we go out for the day, and how I hope she isn't developing a catnip problem we need to worry about.

Laura has never chastised me for tapping my fingers or rubbing my hands in a particular way, never said she's ashamed of me for the way I shake my arms out when I'm anxious, never demanded eye contact to prove I'm paying attention, and never made me feel guilty for the many and various, completely harmless, things my body does that I have limited control over.

Early in 2018 Laura and I moved in together. It was a big change for both of us, and we took a little while to find our routine together. Slowly we worked out what worked for us and what didn't. We worked out who was least bothered by which household chores, and how to arrange our collections of Gundam figures, Transformers, Rubik's cubes, Power Rangers Megazords, and more within our shared spaces.

Our living room is brilliant. It's colorful and vibrant, and full of things we both enjoy doing, and looking at, and playing with. Things that capture our essence. Things that fascinate and delight us as well as our occasional visitors. Things we spent so long having to tidy away or hide because others thought them unseemly or somehow inappropriate.

Just like the parts of ourselves that had previously been tucked away, here they are proudly on display. Without shame, without fear, without judgment. It is a joyous celebration of who we are.

After a social event, we both tend to feel really drained. Be it a three-day convention, a night out at a loud venue, or even a weekend visit from a friend, we both understand that we need to be able to switch off from everything around us and do our own thing. For a while when we first moved in together, one of us would usually go to another room. I don't remember exactly when, but at some point we just started having that recovery period together. We rarely speak during that time, be it a few hours or a whole Sunday, but when it's just the two of us it feels like rest. Every now and then, one of us may hold out a hand, and the other will hold it for a while, but that's the extent of it. There's no social demand, no expectations, no one is being rude by not talking or otherwise interacting, there's no incomprehensible allistic rules about how we're supposed to behave—we just quietly exist together in close proximity. She's my physical-proximity human, my safe space, and knowing we have each other to come home to after being around other people is a warm and gentle joy.

On the two or three occasions we've had emotional conversations, they have been vastly different to those with previous partners. Neither of us expects eye contact as proof that we're paying attention to the other, and if my stutter has started to manifest, Laura has given me as much time as I need to respond, or even suggested alternative methods of communication.

Each of us has expressed our needs, we've discussed how they can be achieved, and we've come to a resolution. The closest we've been to shouting is if one or other of us is struggling with controlling the volume of our voice while under stress, not because being louder means winning the argument. They're not even arguments, just emotional conversations around stress-related problems.

When Laura proposed to me, I momentarily forgot how to speak; I didn't fully process that I hadn't actually said yes. I just flapped my jaw a bit, and excitedly hugged her while happy-crying. Afterwards, she double-checked, and yes, I absolutely wanted to marry her.

We'd actually discussed marriage a few times previously. One of the major parts of those discussions was that we didn't want to spend a lot on rings. We acknowledge that we're clumsy and forgetful, and we will often fidget with things. We understood and accepted that it is more than likely that we would take our ring off to wash our hands and accidently leave it somewhere, or slide it down our finger to fiddle with it and accidentally drop it without noticing. We know that we're disabled, and we made plans to handle that eventuality as painlessly as possible.

I've seen people in extreme distress at losing or damaging their wedding rings. For some it's a fear that this is not just a lost item, but a possible portent for the end of their relationship. When Laura damaged her first ring, I just went upstairs and retrieved a spare that I'd bought, just in case. It was so casual and painless, but for both of us it was a clear display that we mean what we say, there's no unspoken subtext. There's no secret rules that we're supposed to know. No one is going to get angry for the kind of mistakes we make all the time.

Thanks to the space she has given me, to be the way I am without limit, I feel far more comfortable in every aspect of my life. On our wedding day, I bounced, I flapped, I let every weird noise that bubbled up just tumble out, we made puns about small cakes and sandwiches. I wore the unconventional dress, and shoes which calmed my senses.

I danced in the aisles of a really fast train, and went home to lie wordlessly on the couch with my new wife.

Laura has given me the words and understanding and compassion to be unashamedly autistic. That freedom is the greatest joy I could hope for, that's what brings me a real and genuine smile.

Oops, All My Friends Are Autistic

Laura Kate Dale

One of the greatest myths perpetuated by the autism spectrum disorder diagnostic criteria, since the inception of their earliest variations, is the idea that autistic people are, as a rule of thumb, bad at social communication.

Back in the 1970s, a model for simplifying discussions of autism symptoms was developed, called the "triad of impairments." Autism is a spectrum condition, with each person impacted in a variety of varied and unique ways, but the triad of impairments model basically simplified autism as a condition into being about three core pillars—three areas where we, as autistic people, are "fundamentally flawed" compared to our non-autistic peers.

It didn't take into account sensory oversensitivity at all, breaking autism down into being about impaired social imagination, impaired social interaction, and impaired social communication.

The DSM-5 (Diagnostic and Statistical Manual of Mental Disorders, Fifth Edition), a more up-to-date diagnostic manual, instead uses a "dyad of social impairments" model that takes sensory symptoms into account, but still doesn't address my fundamental disagreement with how the impairment model of autism presents social interaction in the autistic community.

Impairment of social imagination, renamed in the dyad as restrictive, repetitive patterns of behavior, is the label given to difficulty with changes in routine, our literal style of thought, our rigid belief systems, and our obsessive areas of hyperfixation. These are all portrayed as negatives, never positive, by their variation from the norm, and explained as an inability to imagine things being different from how they are, or to think in new and novel ways. I disagree with a lot about this, but that would be its own lengthy tangent to get into discussing.

Impairment of social interaction, and impairment of social communication, the two remaining parts of the triad/half of the dyad, are where autistic styles of communication are discussed, purely in clinical and negative terms. Autistic people, according to these impairment models, are incapable of appreciating the social usefulness or pleasure of communication, talk *at* people rather than to them, struggle to express our own feelings or emotions or manage those feelings appropriately, fail to understand the feelings or beliefs of others, struggle to understand appropriate levels of social physical contact as expected and harmless, struggle to understand non-verbal subtext, cannot understand social relationships and hierarchy, struggle to initiate and maintain relationships, and cannot understand social rules.

I am here to say, that is bullshit.

As an autistic person, with a happy and fulfilling social circle full of other autistic and otherwise neurodiverse adults, I can confidently say that most of these impairments are very much written from the perspective of non-autistic clinicians, who view any variation from their own expected socialization standards as disordered behavior, to ideally be fixed rather than embraced or understood.

Autistic people, in many cases, don't struggle to socialize with each other. We struggle to socialize with non-autistic people on their terms, in their unwritten language, due to a lack of tools to facilitate translation of experience.

This is obviously a generalization, but one I have come to firmly believe as I've embraced an understanding of myself through the lens of my autism diagnosis, and been able to fill my social circle with other people who I find easy to understand, and be understood by.

If you let us communicate on our own terms, with each other, autistic people often find communication a lot easier than when we are forced to translate ourselves into a more societally expected "standard."

If autistic people were the majority group by population size, and the non-autistic community were forced to adapt to autistic social rules and expectations, I think they would likely find themselves labelled as struggling to socialize too. The issue wouldn't be that non-autistic people suddenly couldn't socialize, it would be that their socialization style was different from the locally expected norm, and not tailored to cross that social language divide easily. In a situation where they had to grow up without being around many other non-autistic individuals, they would likely feel socially isolated by their separation from expectations.

But I am getting ahead of myself, and talking a little impersonally here. Let's rewind a little, and talk about my own journey with socialization.

Growing up, I struggled to make friends. I wasn't diagnosed as autistic in childhood, and was not put in situations where I was able to knowingly spend time with many other autistic children. There are probably kids I grew up around who had various neurodiverse conditions, but I wouldn't want to speculate about people I remember from decades in my past.

When you look at me as a child, in that setting, the triad of impairments model probably would have looked, from the outside, like it was explaining my experiences pretty well. I spent half of my childhood with one group of 30 peers, then moved schools and spent the second half of my childhood with a second group of 30 kids. Statistically, if we use the commonly stated figure that around 1 percent of the global population is autistic, I probably didn't have any other autistic people in my immediate social circle. If there were others, we were certainly not a significant population of that social setting.

The school education system doesn't leave much room for picking who you socialize with, or gravitating toward people with whom you are a natural fit. You spend eight hours per day, five days per week, sitting with the same people. Much like an office job environment, they are people with whom you have a known starting relationship. They are your social base, and if you lack a common communication style, you are going to struggle socially to connect with the people around you.

The only autistic people I knew, definitively, growing up were members of my extended family. I have close family members I did not grow up living with, but saw semi-regularly, who I found remarkably easy to spend time with. From a young relative whose autism-focused home education lessons I used to take part in because he valued my company and focused better with me involved, to older relatives only now being diagnosed who I found easier to communicate with than my peers as a child, it was clear even before diagnosis that I had an easy time making connections with, and gravitated toward, the autistic people in my life.

For much of my life, struggling to socialize with the peers I was forcibly grouped with in school set me up to think I fundamentally struggled with social communication.

When, in my late teens, I was diagnosed on the autism spectrum, the description given by the triad model made sense to me. I had grown up largely around non-autistic peers, and had struggled to understand how to use social communication effectively. I had struggled with finding joy in the ways I was expected to speak. I had struggled to talk to people in a way they didn't see as talking *at* them, whatever that meant. I felt emotions in different ways to my peers, to different degrees, and struggled to understand why they felt things differently to me. I struggled with the level of physical contact they wanted, and struggled to understand the silently spoken subtext that came to them as second nature. I struggled to understand where I fit in unstated hierarchies, and struggled to initiate and maintain lasting friendships.

But, we're here to talk about where this model falls apart a little, and for me that came many years into my adulthood. For me, it came as a result of being able to start making friends outside of settings where your social circle was predetermined by physical location. Once I started making friends outside of school, and outside of traditional workplace employment, my relationship to socialization began to change too.

A lot of the friends I hold closest to me today were either friend-ships formed online, where I could find people with whom my communication style meshed well regardless of physical distance, or friendships made via mutual friends, people who already got on well with people I got on well with.

I've always found written and text-based communication easier than spoken communication, something that has become increasingly apparent in the digital age. When able to talk using a medium where non-verbal subtext has to be made verbal, a world of emoticons to denote laughter when something is meant sarcastically, or where a tone tag can communicate that same unstated meaning, I could suddenly take part in jokes without worrying so much that I would be misunderstood and cause upset unintentionally through poor delivery. I could take time to make sure my words were correct, without being expected to respond instantly while having to make eye contact and trying to monitor my tone of voice or volume to avoid unintentionally being seen as angry or upset. I could finally strip away a lot of the parts of communication that caused me to conflict with others, and it became much easier to avoid conversations spiraling based on confusion and lack of clarity.

My hyperfixation on specific topics, and my obsessive knowledge about specific niche interests, while not seen as interesting or valid in a setting comprising a random cross section of society who might not share that interest or communication style, were suddenly able to find connection online. I found other people who either loved the things I knew a lot about, or were happy to simply find joy in someone else finding joy, and suddenly my obsessive desire to talk about my favorite things was not a social limitation or impairment, but a key part of how I made connections with others.

While I never sought out autistic people for friendship online, by nature of being autistic, and not shying away from autistic communication styles online, I unintentionally surrounded myself with other autistic people.

Today, my social media following is *very* heavily skewed toward autistic people. My communication style drew in others who communicated the same way I did.

Over the past five or so years, I have made a lot of close, personal friends in the physical world. As said before, some of those friendships started because of the internet, others not. However, important to understand for this story, at the time these friendships began, basically none of them were people who had an autism diagnosis, or any stated belief they might be autistic.

I didn't make friends with these people because I knew they were autistic, and was seeking out friendships with other autistic people. I became friends with these people because, with them, socialization was easy in a way it had never been growing up. These people didn't drain my very limited social battery, and there was something magical about that.

As an autistic person, when I talk about socializing being difficult or tiring, the way I often try to explain it to others is this idea of a social battery. Generally, when socializing with non-autistic people, or people without any neurodiverse conditions, I find myself having to do a reasonable degree of on-the-fly translation of my language, behaviors, and communication styles to match those of who I am spending time with. Doing that work drains a finite resource, which needs time to recharge, and as that tank runs dry, keeping myself appearing non-autistic becomes more challenging.

I first started to make friends who didn't seem to drain this social battery in my early 20s, when I found a group of people who shared my interests in anime and video games. We started traveling to conventions together, dressed up in elaborate costumes, spending days at a time together, with me not needing the same degree of quiet, space, and respite I had always previously found necessary around other people.

I met the woman who is now my wife several years ago, and found the same strange situation with her. Time spent in her company was not a drain on that social battery in the way other humans tend to be. I didn't seem to need to translate myself to be palatable to her. The same goes for friendships I made via her web of social connections, from our local hippy board game friends, to the activist raver, to the queer couple down the seaside who we engage in long-running wargame campaigns with.

In hindsight, a big part of why these friendships felt so easy, and seemed to contradict the social impairment model of autism, was due to the fact that we seemed to share common aspects of communication. We all valued direct communication, being told directly feelings without pretense, double meaning, or secretive hidden intent. We didn't have to explain the nuances of our own lived experiences, as we already understood the examples we would give to each other. We were not expected to apologize for how we were, and had a degree of freedom to be ourselves unapologetically.

It's hard to put into words what it was we were feeling, but we were drawn to each other. We enjoyed speaking with each other, and knew how to communicate in ways that were functional, and achieved what we hoped for. We were not seen as talking *at* each other, we understood that our communication styles were mutual and reciprocal. We understood each other's feelings, and could explain our feelings in ways that would be understood. We understood that physical contact needs differ between individuals, and could sense the signals designed to tell us when a hug needed to end, or not be initiated to start with.

We were able to initiate, and maintain, relationships, while understanding a set of social rules and cues that felt natural to us.

Now is probably the right time to tell the truth about something. While this essay is called "Oops, All My Friends Are Autistic," that's not strictly true. Some of my friends have no diagnosed neurodiversity to speak of, and have no interest in pursuing a diagnosis, despite my suspicions in some cases. Some of my friends have their suspicions that something's up, but are not sure what diagnosis might fit for them. Some of my friends have diagnoses for other conditions I share with them, such as ADHD (attention deficit hyperactivity disorder), and some of them are in the middle of personal revelations about the fact that some of their symptoms might fit better with autism than other diagnoses they received in the past.

To be totally accurate, a lot of my friends are autistic, or have other conditions that have high rates of overlapping occurrence with autism, or have simply lived lives around autistic people, and come into their relationship with me ready to understand, and put in the work needed so that the pressure is not totally on me to cross the neurodiversity communication divide.

Not all of my friends are autistic, but a statistically significant majority are, and the number coming to that realization is growing by the day. In the time since I met many of these wonderful, lovely individuals, a lot of them have come to this realization through conversations with me about my lived experiences. They too have lived their lives struggling socially with others until our little social circles formed, where suddenly socialization came more easily. Many of them have come to realize they are autistic, and that the reason we get on so well, and find each other so easy to be around, is because that level of baseline self-translation is able to fall away.

We found each other, and gravitated together, in part because we found communication free, and easy, for the first time in our lives.

We found people who we didn't find it hard to communicate with, or be understood by.

Without knowing the labels that united us, we found each other.

Autistic people, finding other autistic people.

People with ADHD finding other people with ADHD.

Trans people finding each other, before either side had been ready to come out as trans yet.

Like finding like.

People finding people who inherently and intuitively understood what we were experiencing, and allowed us to let down that wall of self-translation.

The triad and dyad of impairments, as models of observing autism, feel like outside observations. Because, the truth is, once I found other autistic people to connect with, I no longer felt impaired socially, at least while surrounded by those friends, family members, and romantic partners.

Autism is, in many cases, a social impairment by comparison and contrast. When I found a wife I could sit quietly next to, doing my own thing without talking, and not be seen to be ignoring her, not seen as not spending time together because the activities we were doing were different but proximate, everything changed. When I found friends who would be okay with me playing *Pokémon* in our hotel room on holiday, because someone had offered to trade me a shiny Wartortle, and I needed it for my hyperfixation shiny collection I was working on, because they knew how much that meant to me, everything changed. When I found friends I could sit quietly gaming with, not saying a word but sharing an activity with, and still be seen as socially contributing, even if I wouldn't join a group hug in celebration of in-game victory, everything changed.

As an autistic person, I don't struggle to communicate socially. I struggle to communicate with neurotypical people who have not put in the work to see past the idea that my communication style is an issue for me to solve. I struggle to communicate with people who have not put in the work to cross the divide themselves, to see how difficult it can be to communicate in a language not your own.

Once I understood that, the idea that I could have a life full of easy and joyous social connections felt a whole lot less out of reach than my diagnosing physician had always made it seem.

I have a wonderfully supportive group of friends I do not find difficult to be around. Our communication isn't impaired, it's just not the language that most people speak.

From Building a Deck to Building a Community

Aoife Fairweather

"Autistic"—a label I've lived with for most of my life. That's not necessarily a bad thing, self-understanding is helpful, but it has unavoidably colored a lot of my interactions throughout the years.

From the jump I was always apart from my peers in some way, whether it was for additional support or just my own accidental isolation from other kids. I wasn't antisocial per se: if you approached me wanting to talk about my special interest hyperfixations we would become fast friends, but it wasn't easy for me to navigate the quirks of normal conversation.

I learnt from a young age that being noticeably autistic was something I should avoid, and I worked hard to overcome as many of my obvious tells as I could. Due to a combination of my parents and teachers discouraging my autistic behaviors, and other children identifying that there was something "different" about me, I learned early on that autism was something for me to correct, and that would keep others from liking me.

I was ashamed of my autism.

That all changed for me when a game called *Yu-Gi-Oh!* hit the playground. Suddenly not only was my hyperfixation the talk of the playground, it was also the primary driver of social interaction.

For those unaware, *Yu-Gi-Oh!* is a trading card game, based on an animated TV show, where players take on the role of powerful summoners and "duel" each other, with the goal of reducing the other player's life points to zero. This is represented by putting together a deck of cards depicting spells, monsters, and traps that the players battle with. Players get to customize not just the overall gameplay style of their deck, but also the granular specifics that make one variation of a strategy differ from someone else's. One player might build a deck full of aggressive monsters that want to end the game as fast as possible, while another might create a delicate combo deck that can, by playing a specific set of cards, win the game in a single turn. All of this is set to the backdrop of an edgy TV show where heroes with silly hair battle occult forces via said card games (at times on motorcycles).

Unlike a lot of other hobbies, I find that card games are something of an easy mode of social interaction—a hard-coded set of rules to govern your interactions, and a series of scenarios to discuss during and after matches. While not every player who gets into collectable card games goes down the rabbit hole, the fact that to be successful requires selecting 40 cards from a selection of thousands, learning common deck types and their counters, and researching how to exploit niche rulings, means that the players who get invested in doing well at collectable card games often end up needing to acquire the kind of obsessive knowledge that came naturally to me as an autistic child.

I never really got that good at playing *Yu-Gi-Oh!* when I was a kid; the collecting and researching aspect was a lot more engaging for me back then. My spare time was spent looking through online databases at the different themes of cards, and then setting out to collect the coolest ones. Spellcasters, elemental heroes, and cyber dragons were my favorites, and I would wander around the playground trying to trade for the cards I had identified in my various internet deep dives. This translated to me having an encyclopedic knowledge that my peers would often tap into when looking for ways to improve their own decks and strategies.

Without a doubt card games had their hooks in me, and would stick with me for my whole life.

The other kids who struggled to approach me before now had an easy way into my odd ways of thinking. We would discuss the cards, the art, and the show that accompanied all of it. I would show off the hare-brained combos I came up with to the more experienced players, and they would laugh at all the ways the combo could go wrong. Other kids would show off their freshly opened rare cards, and I would rattle off all the different ways you could use them.

Having a shared and deep interest with my peers was fulfilling, and helped me figure out how to speak to them.

While *Yu-Gi-Oh!*'s popularity eventually waned—no childhood phenomenon stays the talk of the playground forever—having had a social safety topic for a while did open the doors somewhat for me. People might not have wanted to discuss my special interest topic anymore, but I at least knew that my peers were people I could talk to, and wouldn't instantly reject talking to me.

In high school, card games were a lot more of a niche hobby, and my own interests shifted away from *Yu-Gi-Oh!*. Different card games took over my interest, most notably a similar game called *Cardfight!! Vanguard*.

To an outsider *Yu-Gi-Oh!* and *Cardfight* are quite similar, but the vastly different mechanics and overall more modern feel of the game drew me in as a teen. Now that I was older I could dive deep into videos and articles about high-level strategies, and apply them to my own gameplay.

My friends (who were also neurodivergent) and I became fiercely competitive, always trying to one-up each other and declare ourselves the best of the best. My "Dragonic Overlord the Great" would be one-upped by my friend's "Ragnaclock Dragon," which would get beat out by another friend's "Commander Lambros." This cycle of playing and improving with each other drove us deeper and deeper into the hobby. Eventually, I wanted to share our group's effort with other people, and I started creating my own *Cardfight* content online based around competitive strategy.

Unfortunately, the day eventually came when I had to move away from those friends and, while we tried to stay in touch, we eventually grew apart. I retreated back into my shell and, now that I was approaching adulthood, the crutch of my fixations really fell away. I didn't have other people around to indulge my interests with, and I struggled to make friends without that shared interest safety topic. I started to feel quite isolated (not exactly helped by a move to a somewhat isolated rural area) and felt the need to look for a community elsewhere.

So I retreated into the online world.

It started with small interactions on the *Cardfight* subreddit, and then posting links to my content there. I had lost my tribe in the real world, but in cyberspace I could find people just as obsessed as I was. Once again, thanks to card games I found a way to overcome the social walls that stood between myself and others.

Eventually I was invited to join Discord chat rooms off the back of my content, full of like-minded players who had found my analysis helpful and had reached out to me directly.

The shift from the slower posting of Reddit and internet forums to the fast-paced real-time chat rooms of Discord was nerve-wracking at first. I was used to having as much time as I needed to think up a response with no expectation of immediacy, and adjusting to the world of instant replies took some deliberate effort. At the same time, it did teach me more about how to express myself in general. I could fall back on my detailed *Cardfight* opinions when a joke didn't land, or I came across awkwardly. The social safety net topic helped me to navigate through that learning process.

This period of trial and error let me develop my own way of speaking, and really find my own sense of humor and footing in real-time conversation.

When unrelated conversations would come up, I felt confident enough in myself that I could join in. Not only did I have my fall-back topic of talking about the game, but I had started to form genuine friendships with the people in the Discord server. It might have seemed like I was quite isolated to outsiders looking in, but through the internet I had forged real relationships with people all over the world.

At some point I moved on from playing *Cardfight*. Changes to the game, and a desire for a more robust competitive experience, sent me down a different path. Nonetheless, the friends I made in those close-knit Discord communities remain strong to this day. The first place I would eventually come out as trans would be in one of those Discord groups, and throughout the pandemic and a period of deep depression they were a lifeline.

(Love you Matt and Jaye.)

Magic: The Gathering though was a new frontier!

Unlike the other games I had played, *Magic* was marketed at an older audience. This meant that it had more complicated and difficult gameplay, and a vast competitive scene. *Cardfight* had a meagre two events a year, and *Yu-Gi-Oh!* hadn't really grabbed my interest for some time. *Magic* on the other hand had weekly high-level events to watch, compete in, and study.

It was exciting to start from almost zero, with a game that had so much history and depth. *Magic* was the first major collectible card game to be released, back in 1993, so I had a lot of catching up to do.

Still, a return to in-person socializing meant a nervous start.

I was terrified that if my mask of practiced normalcy slipped, and the fact I was autistic was revealed to everyone, I would immediately be treated differently. A now ingrained sense of shame towards my autism, and a malformed sense of pride that I could "overcome it," fueled a lot of my early interactions in the *Magic* community.

I know this was perhaps a needless worry—during parts of my childhood my autism had been actively helpful in socializing with others—but trauma runs deep, and isn't always rational. There was still a part of me worried that this time would be different, and I would be corrected or distanced from despite this shared area of interest. Initially I retreated into myself, and focused on building up my skills in isolation. I guess I had a misguided sense that only after earning respect via my playing ability would people look past my eccentricities or quiet awkwardness.

In actuality, the opposite ended up being true.

Being quiet and awkward only made people in the *Magic* community more willing to reach out, to help me improve as a player, and help me feel more welcome. I genuinely could not have found a community more willing to reach out, and try to make sure I felt included. With their support I sharpened my skills, and managed to become a real threat at my local game store.

I was pulled in deeper than ever before, and any moment I had spare was dedicated to becoming a better *Magic* player. Reading articles on ChannelFireball (a *Magic: The Gathering* shop and strategy website), books by Patrick Chapin, and scrutinizing spoilers for powerful new additions to my favorite deck took up most of my free time, and that wasn't even unusual! Everyone I met in the competitive community was like that. To some extent, the obsessive level of dedication required to compete in collectible card games gives you something in common with the autistic community.

It wasn't too long before I managed to make a decent name for myself among the Scottish trading card game/*Magic: The Gathering* community. Eventually people would even come to me for my thoughts on new cards, strategies, and decks. Everyone had their own war stories from events they played previously, or favorite card to ramble on about. There were long debates about how best to build the top standard decks, or who the real greatest of all time was.

I started to feel the mask slipping, I was less afraid to be my true self, and those self-imposed walls didn't seem so tall all of a sudden.

I was there to witness the pure elation the Scottish *Magic* community felt watching the pillar of the local community, Gary Campbell, win the Grand Prix Birmingham tournament, the first Scottish player to achieve this feat.

I had the same nervous excitement at the tension of that one final card draw to decide an important match.

The same frustration as another opponent sat down playing an annoying deck that was good against my own.

Becoming known for playing my precious blue white control strategy was a badge of honor, even more so when more experienced players would ask my opinion on how to play the strategy themselves.

Even the notorious "card flicking" habit that plagues card game players became a soothing way for me to stim during games.

Thanks to my local community I was able to start traveling around Scotland to compete in various qualifier events that would hopefully lead to larger tournaments. One year I even managed to win an event that let me qualify for a special tournament called the European Modern Series Finals.

The Modern finals was part of a circuit that involved smaller qualifiers around the country, the winner of each qualifier earning their invitation for the finals. The tournament was in Stansted, and would mark my first time traveling outside of Scotland for an event. Not only that, it would be a difficult two-format competition, requiring players to complete a booster draft event (an event that requires building a deck from cards opened in randomized packs, which are then passed around the table after a card is selected), before playing the usual constructed rounds using carefully planned decks.

These "usual" rounds would be no slouch though, and were going to be taking place using the popular "Modern" format. Competitive *Magic* is broken up into a variety of "formats," which are essentially card choice restrictions. In the case of Modern, players can choose cards from the past 20 years of the game from which to build their decks. This means that the format supports literally hundreds of different potential strategies, and each one requires different kinds of counterstrategies.

Fortunately, I loved booster drafting, and wasn't half bad at it either, thanks to advice from the legion of older players who had been drafting for as long as the game had been around. Not so fortunately, it was a premium draft format, meaning that the booster packs required to practice for the tournament would cost four times more than regular packs. This meant that the cost of practicing for this event would rack up pretty fast.

During my preparation for this event some people from my local community approached me asking if I wanted to form a testing team with them. Competitive *Magic* involves a lot of practicing against various strategies, testing out different cards and decks against each other to find the best choices for a given tournament. While one option is to play practice matches using an online client like *Magic*

Online or *Arena*, another is to form an in-person testing team with other players.

Testing teams commit to working together to figure things out, alongside taking part in regular testing sessions, putting theories into practice against each other. We shared the dream of one day winning the Pro Tour, and set to work preparing for the upcoming event. We worked together to build up a collection of the cards from the set (called a "cube") that we could use to simulate the experience of drafting, without having to buy packs. As much of our time as we could spare was spent playing and thinking about *Magic*, working together to push each other forward.

Travelling to Stansted itself was an interesting experience. Since I was the only one from my game store to qualify, I initially gravitated towards socializing with the other Scottish players. But again, *Magic* stepped in to fill in the social gaps between myself and other competitors. Despite our differences, I had a great time hanging out with new people, something that a few years prior would have terrified me.

It does sound clichéd, but the way competitive gaming can bring people together sometimes feels...magic.

Eventually, the team decided that we would all travel to Brussels for the upcoming Grand Prix event held there. The brand new "Pioneer" format would be used for the event, and we were all eager to sink our teeth into it.

Pioneer was something of a middle point between the previously mentioned Modern format and the ever-changing Standard format (a format with cards from the last two years). Pioneer contained cards from the last ten years of the game, and being a brand-new format there were a lot of different decks possible within the card pool.

Around this point I began to really suffer from my gender dysphoria. It was something I had carried with me for a long time, and it finally began to overwhelm me.

Magic, and a drive to succeed not just for myself but my teammates as well, helped me through a really rough patch. Being able to pour all my focus into something helped distract me from the debilitating horror of the dysphoria I was experiencing. We tested and trained relentlessly, bringing our laptops to in-person events to play *Magic Online* between real-world rounds. Decks were built and taken apart, wins and losses traded, and hotel plans made. I stayed the course, locking in with my beloved blue white deck before even seeing if it would be a good fit for the new format.

Blue white control felt like an expression of myself at this point, and no other deck, regardless of strength, would suit me better. Something about the fantasy of a mage carefully fending off hordes of creatures and deflecting powerful spells really spoke to me. On top of that, something about a deck built around controlling the game felt right, when I felt like I was losing control of everything else in my life. It probably wasn't the best deck for the event, but it was the best deck for me dammit!

Honestly, I was so focused on the fact I was going to get to play *Magic* that I didn't even realize that Brussels was in Belgium (I am not good at geography). It wasn't until we were at the airport that I excitedly realized I could get some genuine Belgian chocolate.

Apart from excitedly riding all forms of Brusselian public transport, we were singularly focused on *Magic: The Gathering*, in a room with hundreds of people all passionately excited about exactly the same thing. On the day of the event I could barely even think about my own drive to win; genuinely, I was driven by my friends. I wanted to show that our practice was worth it, and after losing two rounds early on in the tournament, I was in a position where any loss would knock me out of the event. Still, I wanted to prove that we were the real deal, and the moments between rounds where I would find my friends and wordlessly high five them to tell them I was still alive were worth fighting for.

Unfortunately, a draw in the final round meant I couldn't proceed to day two, but I nonetheless felt like I had proved that our fledgling team was no joke.

Seven hundred miles from home, in a body that felt wrong and surrounded by people I had never met, I felt at home. All of a sudden those "shameful" autistic traits I worked so hard to "overcome" were all positives among my new peers. Hiding my autism started to seem more and more ridiculous, and I started to be open about it. When people would make an ableist comment born from ignorance, I would step in to explain their missteps and they would listen and apologize for their mistakes.

I realized that my autism was just another aspect of myself—why would I need to somehow triumph over that?

All of a sudden there were no walls at all.

It's an odd experience to realize that your own perception of yourself was just a shield against harm, and to start unravelling yourself from the safety blanket around your own heart.

But...

The shame was gone.

And this gradual process of accepting my autism helped lead to an acceptance of my gender, so I started my transition. It had been something brewing inside me for a long time, and I had definitely hit the point of no return. Through competitive card gaming I had become more confident in myself, and felt ready to start really being myself. It wasn't easy, but thanks to the real friends I had made, from long-distance confidants to close friends made through competition, I finally felt ready.

When the pandemic hit, our team's dream of qualifying for the next pro-tour got put on hold, and eventually slipped away altogether. It might seem a little cliche but what we had actually achieved was worth more than a premier tournament.

Over the course of the pandemic we went from being "Magic friends," to genuinely close friends.

I no longer needed the safety net that card games had once provided, and I felt so much more confident in myself, my gender, my autism, and just generally being myself without apologizing. What once was a point of shame is now something I'm even comfortable cracking jokes about and discussing openly.

I have not lost the urge to compete with others, but I've since moved on to fighting games as an outlet for my competitive drive.

While it might sound sad that I have moved on from trading card games, it's really not. At the end of the day, it was never specifically trading card games I found joy in, it was games. Games with high complexity, lots of stats to learn, and a skill ceiling I could let my autistic brain latch onto learning and excelling at. That's my source of joy, and while the specifics may shift, I will always be the kind of person who loves climbing the skill ladder at complex games.

The mindset I built up playing competitive card games has been a great asset for me as I dive into fighting games. The careful iteration of strategy, and deep well of information to study and build upon, have a lot in common with my former interests. Not just that, the confidence I built up let me put myself forward without shame, apology, or fear. I've forged new bonds with new sorts of people, and now that the walls are down I don't think they'll ever be up again.

Who cares if my thought process is a little outside of the norm? I can't be anyone else, after all. It's not just that I've found places where I can be myself—I've found out how to be myself no matter what.

I'm me.

And I've never been happier!

The New Dress

C. N. Josephs

A genderfluid writer living in Seattle, WA
with his spouse and spoiled Pomeranian.

One fall afternoon in 2021, my fiancé Nick asked me, "Hey, baby, what do you want for Christmas this year?"

I had to pause and turn that over. At the best of times, I've never been good at answering that question; the second someone asks me what kind of gifts I'd like, I immediately forget everything I've ever wanted. And this certainly wasn't the best of times—my stepdad had died of a stroke recently, and in my haze of grief, I think I genuinely forgot that Christmas was coming up. But, after thinking on it for a few minutes, something came to me:

As an autistic person with high sensory needs, I have to be picky about the clothes I wear—the wrong fabric, or a scratchy tag, or an annoying seam can quickly lead to me getting overwhelmed and having a breakdown. When I find clothes that do meet my particular needs, I latch onto them and wear them for years, well past the point that I should have thrown them out.

This was the case for The Dress.

The Dress was a sundress from Torrid: spaghetti straps, knee-length, light purple, decorated with a floral pattern. While it was meant for the summer, I loved it enough to wear it even in cold weather by pairing it with leggings and a sweater. I had owned it for years, and it was showing its age—the print was barely visible, the color had faded to grey, and it was covered in rips and stains. It was still a good sensory experience, so I refused to throw it out, but it was getting harder to ignore that it was rapidly becoming unwearable.

"I want a replacement for my purple sundress," I told Nick. "I know you won't be able to find the exact one—I've already looked, Torrid doesn't carry it anymore—but something as close as possible, please."

Nick looked at me with something in their face that I couldn't quite read—like they were plotting something. They slowly smiled and said, "Alright. I can do that."

As much as you want it to, life doesn't stop for grief, and I had to dive into Christmas preparations soon after that. Within a few days, I was so caught up in holiday planning that I forgot about my request for a new dress. I knew that the first Christmas without my stepdad was going to be rough for my family, and I wanted to make it better, for myself and the rest of my family. Without fully realizing it, I started slipping into harmful coping methods that became entwined with me during childhood: I ignored my own needs to take care of my family instead.

The tricky thing about growing up autistic is that when your needs don't make sense to your caregivers, they can end up viewing those needs as unimportant. "I can't stand bright lights, big crowds, or loud noise" doesn't make sense to someone who's never had a breakdown in a grocery store. "I need to do things a particular way or I'll freak out" doesn't make sense to someone who can change their routine at a moment's notice. So the message I received consistently throughout my childhood was that my needs didn't matter.

Add in the way that I was made to feel responsible for taking care of everyone else in my family, and I ended up with a deep-seated belief that taking care of my own needs is selfish, and the morally right thing for me to do is ignore them to take care of everyone else. I've spent years in therapy trying to shed those beliefs, but...grief has a way of making your old bad habits come back with a vengeance. So now, it seemed only natural that I would do whatever was necessary to give my family the perfect Christmas—even if I had to ignore my own needs to do it.

Here's the list of tasks I gave myself:

1. November–December: Do an ungodly amount of Christmas shopping, make 16 homemade gifts, individually wrap 115 presents, and plan the perfect Christmas dinner for 15 people.

2. December 23: Drive five hours to the other side of the state to celebrate Christmas with Nick's family in Walla Walla.

3. December 26: Drive back to Seattle and have the aforementioned perfect Christmas dinner.

Despite the stress I was under, things weren't completely awful. I had Nick. When we met working on a play together in 2015, I was immediately drawn to them.

Have you ever met someone and just known from your first conversation that they were going to be in your life for a long time? That's what

I felt with Nick: that nearly indescribable feeling of "You and I must be made from the same batch of starstuff." Or, maybe it's nothing so mystical. Maybe it's just "I like you enough to put in the effort to choose you every day, even when it's hard."

Part of it, I think, is that Nick and I are both trans and neurodivergent. That's not all there is to a good relationship, of course—there are trans neurodivergent people I can't stand and cis neurotypical people I adore—but it helps. Having a partner who shares your fundamental experiences makes it easier for them to understand you. And, after a lifetime of being hurt by a family member who said that my autistic traits embarrassed her and that I couldn't be transmasculine because I had "feminine energy," having someone who just got it was like the relief of a drowning man getting his first gasp of air.

I would later learn that through all of this, Nick was hard at work on their own Christmas task—the plan that started taking form when I first mentioned The Dress.

As absorbed as I was in my own to-do list, I didn't even notice what they were up to. I was hyper-focused on crafting, wrapping, planning; whatever I needed to do to make Christmas good for my family. I had no idea that Nick was hard at work to make sure that Christmas was good for me, too.

There were various points during this period when Nick (being a kind and loving partner) did try to tell me that I was going too hard and should rest. But I (being as stubborn as a wine stain on white carpet) insisted that I was fine. I had it in my head that I was solely responsible for ensuring that my family had a good Christmas, even if it meant I was falling apart.

And then December 23 came, and it was time to go across the state to Walla Walla. At this point, I was so exhausted that the idea of going to a largely unfamiliar city to spend several nights in a house that wasn't mine seemed like torture. But we hadn't visited Nick's family in years, and I knew how much they were looking forward to seeing us, so I pushed myself to go.

Even in Walla Walla, we weren't able to rest: we still had unfinished Christmas gifts to make and wrap. But now, we didn't have the comforts of our home, our predictable routine, and our own familiar bedroom to retreat to at the end of the day. The first night was okay, but the next night—Christmas Eve—we both crashed hard. We ended up curled up together in the guest bedroom in their mom's basement, just sobbing and clutching onto each other. We were finally finished making and wrapping gifts, but now all that we wanted in the world was a chance to celebrate Christmas with just each other, in our own home.

The idea of doing something that makes other people sad just because it benefits me has always been terrifying. But here, crying with my partner, I had my first moment of clarity in weeks: I need to do what's best for me right now. I cautiously brought up the idea of leaving a day early so that we could have a chance to have our own private Christmas celebration at home. I knew it might disappoint Nick's family to have us leave so soon, but maybe that was okay. Nick—looking immediately relieved—agreed.

When I woke up the next morning, a new sense of calm had washed over me. For the first time in weeks, my chance to rest was nearly in my grasp. Nick and I had a lovely Christmas morning with their family, then bid our farewells and hightailed it back across the mountains.

That evening, we unpacked, changed into our pajamas, and fell asleep in our own bed with the comforting knowledge that we could sleep in tomorrow and have an easy morning. Laying there, with my soon-to-be-spouse across from me, our obligations almost over, I was finally able to rest peacefully.

After breakfast the next morning, we sat in front of our little artificial tree to open presents. By this point, with everything that had been going on, I had completely forgotten how I responded all those weeks ago when Nick asked me what I wanted for Christmas. But then I picked up a present that I recognized by size and shape as a garment box, and my request for a new dress came back to me. I ripped into the box, eager to see what they had found. I froze.

Inside the box was a new version of The Dress—clean, unfaded, never worn, still with the tags on. I handled it with the reverence of a priest holding a holy shroud. The texture, the pattern, all of it was exactly the same. Not "a close match," but perfect. My voice was choked with tears as I asked Nick where they found it. They explained that they scoured eBay until they found the exact right dress in my size. I couldn't help but start crying.

I spent so much of my life hiding my autistic traits because I was made to feel deeply ashamed of them—like they were inherently wrong and bad. But the thing about autism, at least for me, is that it's entirely inseparable from who I am as a person. I would still be more or less the same person if I wasn't physically disabled, if I wasn't depressed, if I wasn't anxious. But if you pressed a button and made it so I wasn't autistic, I would be a completely different person. I wouldn't be me anymore.

My autism is a fundamental part of who I am, and I spent so long feeling like there was something wrong with me because of it. But here was my lover, my best friend, telling me that they loved, respected, and cherished my autism, and suddenly all of that barely mattered.

They could have just found any other dress—I'm sure that, at the time of this story happening, Torrid had at least one or two similar dresses on sale. They could have found something that was a close enough match. But they looked at me, and they said, "I know how hard giving up your dress is for you, I know that it feels like hell, and I love you and want to ease that burden, so I'm going to look high and low until I find you the exact same dress."

If we hadn't already been engaged, I would have proposed then and there.

As it was, I just cried and hugged them, and kissed them all over their face.

A few hours after that, we went to have Christmas dinner with my family. I didn't wear The Dress, terrified that the lack of coordination my autism gives me would lead to me spilling something on it the same day that I received it. But I thought about it frequently, hanging up in our closet, ready for me to wear it again and make new memories in it.

Because that's part of it, isn't it? That's part of why I—why so many autistic people—have trouble throwing clothes away. It's not just about the clothes, it's about the memories, the familiarity. When I looked at The Dress, I didn't see its stains or faded pattern.

I saw the warm spring evenings when Nick and I would go to the local you-pick blueberry farm and wander around the trails, sneaking blueberries into our mouths with the care of jewel thieves, as if our blue-stained fingers wouldn't give us away to anyone who saw us.

I saw the hot summer afternoons when Nick and I would go to Alki Beach and stay there until late at night, reading tarot cards by electric candlelight until we got tired and went back to their house to sleep in the same bed together—so desperate for closeness, so hesitant to part from each other, even before we started dating.

I saw the ferry rides we would take out to the San Juan Islands on warm days; I felt how the dress's skirt would blow around my legs on the ferry deck, how its thin fabric would offer me relief from the sweltering heat as we traversed through forests and small towns.

I saw the three years of friendship I had with Nick before we started dating, all culminating in that first shy kiss and the slow blossoming of our romantic relationship. I saw that beautiful June day when we went to the beach to celebrate their birthday and they asked me to marry them.

I saw a map of all the moments where our lives intertwined, from that first play rehearsal to the day they proposed, and all of the beautiful stops in between.

Sometimes a dress is just a dress, but sometimes a dress is a storybook spelling out the most precious moments of your life. Is it any wonder that's hard to get rid of?

The New Dress didn't have those memories exactly, but it was close enough that I'd carry the reminder of them with me wherever I went. And it had a new, even more important memory: the Christmas that could have been the worst one of my life which instead ended up as one of my most precious.

It's impressive, looking back on it now, how such a small action completely turned my Christmas around. When I think back to that time, the stress and anxiety and giant to-do list have faded as neatly as the pattern on the original dress—dulled enough by time to be barely recognizable unless you know what you're looking for. Instead, when I think back to Christmas 2021, my first memory is of The New Dress.

At Christmas dinner with our family, I was happier than I had been in weeks. I felt the absence of my stepdad—we all did—but the peals of laughter outnumbered the bursts of tears, and we all managed to have a good time together. The gifts were thoughtful, the smiles were plentiful, and the food was delicious.

The family member who used to berate me for my autism and transmasculinity was there. Our relationship had calmed down in recent years, and she has stopped saying ableist and transphobic things to me—but, because she never really apologized for any of it and never acknowledged she had done anything wrong, I often found myself tensing up around her, waiting for her to say something that would ruin the shaky peace we've forged.

At one point during dinner, she asked Nick and me how our Christmas had been going, and I cautiously told her about The New Dress: how I was hesitant to get rid of the old one, how much it had meant to me, and the lengths Nick went to get an exact replica. I don't know whether she entirely got the significance of it, but she reacted well and expressed appreciation for how thoughtful Nick was, and that was more than enough for me.

The dinner was still hard at points—I don't think I'll ever be a fan of loud, crowded events. The small living room all 15 of us were crammed into meant that there was always someone within a foot of me, and every bit of sound in the room felt like it was being blared directly into my ears.

But it was bearable because Nick was there. Nick, who knows just how to calm me down, just how to pull me back from the edge of a meltdown before I go toppling off. Nick, who always knows the exact right thing to say at the exact right moment to keep me calm. Nick, who sees my autism and loves me for it.

Despite the shame that people have tried to make me feel, I've spent the past several years carefully cultivating a positive relationship with my autism: working on not just tolerating it, but outright loving it. Stories like this make it a lot easier. If I wasn't autistic, I don't think I would prize the dress as much as I do now for its silky-smooth texture, for the gentle pressure of the fitted bodice, for the way that the spaghetti straps leave my arms free to move as I please. For the memories that rush back when I look at it.

If I wasn't autistic, I think that Nick's gesture of hunting down this dress would be appreciated, certainly, but it wouldn't make me feel a surge of love so overwhelming as to nearly drive me to tears. And a few months later, at our beautiful Pagan wedding in the woods, I don't think the dress would have been on my mind, as a constant reminder that I was making the best decision of my life.

I love my autism. Sometimes, when the negative symptoms rear up, it feels like it doesn't love me back. But other times, when my autism allows a profound feeling of joy that none of my allistic friends fully understand, it feels like my autism is my brain's love letter to my heart: a letter that says, you will experience hardship because of this, but you will also experience unparalleled joy. And because of those moments—because of the autistic joy that my brain gives me as a gift—I wouldn't give up my autism for the world.

Making My Special Interest Hyperfixation into a Career

Laura Kate Dale

Back when I was a very young child, I thought I knew what I wanted to do with my life. Like many kids, largely imagining the world of work through the lens of jobs that came with attached cartoon characters or plastic toys, I wanted to be an astronaut.

Now, looking back as an adult, I get why I idolized the job conceptually. I struggled to connect emotionally with my non-autistic peers, and was pretty relentlessly bullied for being "the weird kid" in class. The idea of getting on a rocket ship and flying as far away as possible from the earth, to a quiet void where none of the world's problems could reach me, was deeply appealing.

I didn't fit in on earth, but maybe if I went out into the stars, I could find some alien species out there to emotionally connect with in that way I craved, but struggled to achieve.

Maybe I was myself an alien, separated from my own species by some freak accident, fallen down to a planet whose customs did not fit.

Maybe, if I could just leave the planet's atmosphere, I would find a place where I belonged.

Now, as you can undoubtedly guess by the fact I am sitting here writing this essay on earth, and not from a floating laptop on the International Space Station, I never ended up pursuing my dreams of being a professional astronaut. A combination of my being disabled, and living in a country with no space program of its own, made it clear pretty quickly that I wasn't ever going to go and find that planet hiding just behind the moon full of aliens who understood me. Unless I someday win the lottery, or find myself a billionaire benefactor willing to finance my seat on a commercial space venture, I doubt that particular dream will ever come to pass.

Still, in my own little way, I did end up finding a job that let me explore strange new worlds, and connect with people meaningfully, all without having to work day to day around people who didn't understand my autism-based peculiarities, or in an environment full of sensory chaos.

Ever since I can remember, I have had a very obsessive interest in video games. In particular, video games with huge sprawling worlds, grand stories, and obsessive amounts of collectables to organize, memorize, and repetitively seek out.

I was born in the early 1990s, and had my first experience with the *Pokémon* games on the original Gameboy at a fairly pivotal point in my childhood. I was eight years old when *Pokémon Red* and *Blue* first released in the UK. I was old enough to have started school, and had experienced several years of struggling to connect socially with my peers. I was young, but I was old enough to understand I was different from other people, and that my nameless difference was a barrier to emotional connections. I think, in part, that's why the release of those games impacted my life the way that it did.

For me personally, one of the key ways my experience of autism is defined is by obsessive and methodical set collection, something the *Pokémon* series was perfectly primed to provide. There were 151 creatures to collect, each only spawned in certain areas, learned certain moves at specific levels, evolved at certain levels, and learned unique moves if evolution was delayed, as well as secrets hidden throughout their world.

My brain was ready to soak up, and obsessively memorize, every bit of data it could.

I came into my love of the *Pokémon* video games as the series was hitting the cultural zeitgeist. It was, for a time, the biggest media property in the world, and my encyclopedic knowledge of the minutiae of the series was, for a time, a social safety net topic for me.

I struggled with social communication, but suddenly I knew a lot about something that people wanted to know. I could tell my friends that Graveller needed to be traded to evolve into Golem, or that Gloom required a Leaf stone to evolve, or that evolving a Pikachu in *Yellow* was impossible, unless you traded a different Pikachu from a different version of the game.

My obsessive fanaticism was a benefit, not a hindrance. People wanted to talk to me, even if it was transactional. If I was struggling to make conversation with someone new, I knew I had *Pokémon* as a topic I could fall back on to keep conversation flowing. I had people who considered me friends.

This didn't last forever of course—popular trends come and go, but video games never lost that special place in my heart over the years, as a topic I knew lots about, and that could in the right circumstances help me to connect with my non-autistic peers.

It took a long time for me to really understand how to make use of that knowledge, but we will get to that in due time.

For much of my childhood, video games were an escapist fantasy, and a coping mechanism for a disability I did not know I was living with. They allowed me to go on grand adventurous quests where I was the hero, off to save the day. Everyone would say their predictable lines, I knew my place in the story, and everyone needed my help.

I was valuable, and I was wanted.

I could obsessively hunt for the same creatures over and over, replay the same plots, and roleplay having a social life where I mattered, in a predictable and safe environment.

The *Pokémon* series in particular became a comfort obsession, evolving in how I interacted with it over time.

As the years went on I began obsessively hunting for Shiny *Pokémon*, special color-swapped variants of creatures that had a roughly 1:4000 chance of appearing while playing. Obsessively walking around in circles hunting these rare variant creatures became a form of socially acceptable stimming for me, a predictable repetitive task I could engage in to calm myself after a stressful or overwhelming day.

While I loved playing video games growing up, at my core, I always wanted to be talking about them as much as, if not more than, I actually wanted to be playing them. For all the joy they brought me, I always found myself drifting back to memories of being eight years old, playing *Pokémon*, but also talking about my love of the game every day, and using that to make friends and connect with other people.

I left school without much in the way of qualifications, or future prospects. The reduction in routine stability that came with secondary school education in my teens was hard for me to handle, and I dropped from being a very academically promising student, to a disabled burnout, over a matter of years.

Still, through it all, a love of video games remained.

When I was around 16, I discovered that "video game critic" was a job that people in the world had. I guess I must have known that at some earlier point—I grew up reading video game magazines and websites regularly and knew people had to write the text in them—but it wasn't until I turned 16 that I really internalized the fact that real human beings out there in the world got paid to talk about video games, and why they feel the way they do about specific ones.

I remember stumbling on a video game podcast hosted by gaming website IGN, focused on Nintendo video games and systems. The two hosts were people, with names, who just sat at a microphone, talking to each other about video games, and someone, somewhere, was paying them to do that.

They were getting paid to talk about a subject they knew inside and out, and wanted to spend their lives focused on.

Maybe, I dared to consider, that could be me someday.

Trying to carve out a career in the video game industry was, to put it lightly, not an easy task. I was not particularly experienced as a writer, my work struggled on a technical level, and the career field is, and was, swarmed with writers willing to work for free for their shot at making video game critique their career. Press events were often sensory overwhelming affairs, and it was tough to form a schedule when opportunities were scarce and often offered suddenly.

It wasn't a career I could guarantee would work out, but it was all I could consider.

I spent many years throughout my early 20s working a stressful and sensory overwhelming day job, doing my best to avoid burnout and meltdown, before coming home and writing. I used my days working in a supermarket to think of ideas for opinions features about video games I could talk about. I wrote, and I wrote, not caring if anyone read or listened. I wrote with every spare moment I had, because it felt good to infodump on a topic about which I had spent my life learning everything I could. It felt good to talk about the things I obsessed over, and hoped that it reached someone.

It felt like I was a lighthouse, shining out my light, in the hopes somebody would notice, and shine theirs back.

I won't get too much here into the minutiae of how I eventually turned unpaid writing into a stable career. That's a story that involves a lot of luck, a lot of grind, and a lot of brute force. I wrote interesting articles, the right people noticed my work at the right time, and I got my big break at a time in my life where I could take a risk on accepting it. At the end of the day, I wrote, and I wrote, and I wrote, until eventually those other lighthouses began to shine their lights back.

When I eventually started to reach a point as a writer where other people were reading my work, or listening to me speak, it felt exactly how I remembered feeling back when I was eight years old, and my obsessive knowledge of *Pokémon* meant that people wanted to talk to me. I had a social safety net topic, and the internet allowed me to find the kind of people who wanted to hear me write myself onto the page. No matter how niche the topic I wanted to enthuse over, there would be someone out there in this big wide world who cared about it too.

I was able to talk about the things I loved, and people wanted to start conversations with me, to discuss their thoughts too. It was opening up dialogue. I was connecting with people.

Writing opinions about video games has been my full-time job now for around eight or nine years. Any time I am asked about the best part of this job, I don't answer by talking about the free early video games I get to play, or the creators I get to speak with. When I think of why I love this job, I think about my life as an autistic person, and the joy that came from managing to make my hyperfixation into a career.

I think about the fact that I get to work from home, in an environment where I can control the sensory experience around me far more than a traditional workplace would allow.

I think about the fact that I have full control of my own work schedule, and can create a predictability and routine that I can work within.

I think about the fact that I can spend my days focusing on the things

I love to obsess over, and that it's then my job to talk about what I think, and explain why I feel the way I do.

I think about the connections I get to make with other people, made easier by the distance of online communication.

When I think back to my childhood desire to be an astronaut, I recall that I wanted that largely because I felt overwhelmed and misunderstood on earth. I couldn't imagine a world where my obsessive interests could be useful, or desirable, or a gateway to human connection.

I don't think I need to be an astronaut anymore. I think I've carved out a corner of connection and stability right here on earth.

Rediscovering Myself

Teagan Rose-Bloid

An anxious, autistic asexual born and raised in the Southeast United States.

I didn't even realize that I was wearing a mask until I had the space to take it off.

I was 21 years old by the time I first speculated that I might be autistic. My mother was working with autistic children at her local school and, suddenly, all those stories about me in my toddlerhood weren't just weird, quirky behaviors and silly situations, but frankly enormous flashing neon signs. And there I was, in the middle with all the arrows pointing at me, looking around and wondering how the hell no one noticed.

To say that the revelation changed my life would be a bit of an understatement. After tearing through resources and personal stories compiled by other autistic people, it was like finally figuring out that the reason you can't unlock your front door is because you're using the wrong key on the ring. Finally, you get inside after freezing your butt off on the stoop for an embarrassingly long time, and you feel the warmth start to seep back into your cheeks, your fingers, the tips of your ears, and you can take off your shoes and start to get comfortable again.

The end of a situation you didn't know was miserable until it was finally over. This isn't what life has to be. Things can be better.

That's not to say there weren't challenges that came with diagnosis. After nearly two decades of living without that single piece of very helpful information, I felt a lot of uncertainty about myself, and who I was meant to be. I ticked a lot of the boxes when I read through possible autism criteria, but I initially felt like I needed to tick all of them for the diagnosis to be my truth.

It took me some time to understand that autism is a spectrum. Not every one of us has every symptom, every trait, to the same degree. Each of us is our own unique mosaic. But, also, when you spend so long being unable to express parts of yourself, for fear of punishment or ridicule, it can be almost as if those parts never existed.

You have to uncover those parts of yourself again. You have to dig them back up from where you buried them. You have to revisit all the things you stopped doing because you were made fun of or corrected, and you have to face all that shame and embarrassment all over again. It might take years to let go of all that baggage, to relearn all the traits that you smothered for the comfort and ease of everyone else.

It's a process, but it's worth it.

Apparently it's a pretty common experience among autistic people—learning you're autistic and then giving yourself a little bit more room to be autistic. That's how it happened for me. Everything clicked into place and I started to think, "Well, if this kind of thing helps autistic people, will it help me?" "If this brings a lot of autistic people joy... will I enjoy it, too?"

Honestly, that's one of the best parts about this period of self-discovery. It was like really seeing myself for the first time. I was unfamiliar, but not in a frightening way. I was one of those excavation toys, a big block of rocks and sand that has little plastic dinosaur bones inside. All I had to do was take up my chisel and start picking away at the shell until I started to find the treasure buried in the center. For the first time in my life, I wasn't afraid of what I'd find. I actually wanted to know. And, again, for the first time in my life, I had the space to explore.

I had just left university after many weeks of struggling against bureaucracy, and three years of trying to willpower myself through the trials of academia. All of it had been without my autism diagnosis, or the diagnosis for my math-related learning disability. There came a time when I realized that I couldn't do it anymore, not for another second, so I finished that semester and I moved in with my partner and their partner. Neither of them are neurotypical, so it was easy for them to give me plenty of breathing room to figure out what my autism meant for me.

I was happy, even excited, to explore this newly discovered aspect of myself, even if it was challenging. Having them there by my side to support and encourage me was paramount. For the first time, I really felt that it was okay, not only to be struggling, but to admit that I was struggling. To admit that I needed space, and time, and gentleness. With their help, the excavation truly began, and part of that excavation was rediscovering all those things that I'd buried out of embarrassment or shame. They helped me learn that I was allowed to love this part of myself even if it was something that so many people had found unfavorable. I was allowed to seek out positive experiences that were unique to me. Unique to autistic people like me.

Previously, through most of my life, a lot of sensory experiences were overwhelming for me, too intense, distressing, or uncomfortable. The world isn't a place where you can always pick and choose what kind of input you're going to get. Up until that point in my life, I'd mostly been coping with sensory processing issues by willpower alone, not understanding that the following bouts of panic, crying, or complete emotional shutdown were a response to being harmed by sensory data which is less invasive for the average person. Once I understood what was happening, I was finally able to turn all that on its head.

Now, with safe exploration enabling me to find my boundaries, and therefore find indulgence, the unique way that my brain processes sensory information is probably the best part about my being autistic. Now, I can work through the difficult parts, and more easily find shortcuts to the positives, to sources of calm, delight, and even outright joy.

The right kind of music, for example, is an incredibly easy shortcut. I don't know if I can properly describe what the "right" kind of music for me is, but with a nice set of headphones there are some sounds that can bring me to a very emotional state. Sure, that's a typical human experience, that's what music is supposed to do, right? But a lot of my enjoyment of music comes from how the sounds feel on the inside of my head. There's a specific kind of sound that "slides," almost like letting something gently slip through your fingers. There are specific notes that, when combined, replicate a smooth, consistent, pleasant sensation. Sometimes sounds can even have a taste—though that detail is probably a result of synesthesia. While it isn't inherently linked to autism, a fair number of autistic people also have this condition wherein sensory information sometimes overlaps. This causes strange misfires in the brain and results in sensory input being processed incorrectly, connecting sight to taste or audio to physical sensation.

To give an example of music that has that feeling, that smoothness, try listening to the Undertale Original Soundtrack. The composer, Toby Fox, uses a small handful of core melodies, and then remixes them constantly, in familiar but slightly different variations. This creates an entire album where there's both a consistent familiarity, which my autistic mind craves, and unexpected differences to keep things feeling fresh.

One of the reasons I believe the *Undertale* soundtrack is particularly interesting to me, in the context of my autism, is that Fox uses a lot of "microtones" in the album. Microtones are notes that exist between the notes of a typical instrument, requiring said instrument to be off-key, or for the note to be replicated on a computer. This creates not only a lot more avenues for creative songwriting, but also much more depth, smoothness, and intrigue. It's a perfect example of the "good kind of music": tunes that ring just right, that bounce and snap, that slide into each other in an incredibly pleasing fashion.

Listen to "Heartache" from that album, and experience a particular rhythm that feels like sadness and uncertainty, that tastes like grief and pleading. Listen to "Metal Crusher" for the confusing but upbeat sensation of being trapped in a deadly game show. Listen to "Undertale" to have all of your emotions put in a blender and turned into soup. Not only is the soundtrack masterful in terms of musical construction, it's an absolute dream for someone like me. A lot of music that is specifically composed for video games can tick the boxes I'm looking for, because they're designed to evoke a certain response from the player, but for me none do it quite so easily and so seamlessly as Toby Fox's compositions. His melodies stick in my head like taffy to teeth.

Music that tickles that part of my brain tends to get stuck between the cogs. Earworms are something that everyone experiences—we've all had a song stuck in our head, we've all had our brains latch on and play something over and over until we're sick of it—but I find that most often I'll find myself drawn to a tiny part of a song.

Most people don't hyperfocus on, for example, a single triplet of notes that sounds nice next to each other. Most people won't loop a song from second 15 to second 20 just to hear a particular lilt in the background. That kind of indulgence is best left for private headphone time, because no one else in the house needs to listen to that, even if they understand that I'm enjoying it.

This is especially true in my household, where myself and another person are earworm-incarnate.

Echolalia is a pretty common autistic trait, but our sister neurotype of attention deficit hyperactivity disorder (ADHD) often shares it. To explain echolalia simply: it's an automatic call-and-response. The call doesn't have to be anything specific, it just has to ping the right way to elicit the unsolicited response. Its most defining characteristic is that the people who experience it often have no filter, no real control over when it activates. They hear something and they repeat that something, automatically, sometimes without even realizing they've done it.

I'm one of them.

So, let me lay out a scenario. Imagine that you're sitting at your dining table with two of your best friends, innocently enjoying your meal. Friend One says something in a silly little voice. It means nothing to you and goes right over your head. Then, Friend Two repeats that phrase in a slightly different silly voice. Friend One responds again with an even sillier voice. This continues anywhere from five seconds to several minutes, with you as a confused metaphorical volleyball net.

This is the life of my partner.

I imagine that it must feel the same to any parent who foolishly bought their child a Furby and then had to listen to that horrible little gremlin voice repeat all the phrases their child had taught it.

(I'm not saying that autistic people are Furbies but that's exactly what I'm saying.)

At the very least, the potential annoyance is balanced out by the objective humor, at least for us. Certain tones of laughter are a 100 percent hit rate. In a bad mood? Quick, say, "Here comes the boy" loud enough to carry across the house, and I'll be there to yell it back in a way more goblin-y voice. Say the word "okay" and I'll pass it back in the cutesy AI voice from the video game *Tacoma*.

Echolalia was previously something that I found really confusing and embarrassing—it just happens, and because it sometimes comes off like you're mocking someone, it can make people upset. I'm grateful that, at least in the safety of my own home, it can be a source of silliness and humor rather than something to worry about.

Speaking of "the safety of my own home," I can admit that I've put my housemates in a bit of a silly situation in regard to communicating with me versus communicating with other people. You see, one of the first autistic traits that I relearned was communication through sound instead of words. Sometimes it's easier to honk in distress than to say anything about being distressed. Sometimes it's easier to get someone's attention with a quick, short sound than to say their name. I suffer from selective mutism pretty intensely, but it's mostly triggered by stress. This, along with learning some basic American Sign Language, has been a way to get around that.

In the past few years, however, it's like my family has developed a new language—one that's predominantly just noise. While I'm not likely to interact with strangers in my day-to-day life, my housemates have to go to work and talk to people. One day my spouse came home and told me, in a weary voice, "I can't talk to normal people anymore," because they had almost responded to someone at work with my characteristic "but I don't want to do that" sound.

These days, my spouse is so good at interpreting me that I can go a whole day without speaking a single word. Let me tell you, that is what love feels like, for me as an autistic person.

That safety has also allowed me to slowly relearn something very intrinsic to being autistic. Stimming. The act of offloading excess stimuli or stress, a self-soothing behavior that can help one refocus and calm down.

There are stories of me stimming as a very young child, but almost none after a certain age. I don't have to tell you that I was bullied in school for my unusual repetitive movements—that's kind of The Official Backstory™ of most autistic people—so a lot of my stimming behavior vanished.

At least, it took on forms that were harder for others to notice.

I picked up teeth-grinding as an acceptable, easily hidable method to self-soothe. I picked that up after I managed to drop finger-biting. Now, I'm trying to transition again, to things that are a bit less destructive.

I have soft, silicone creatures in my desk (like the ones you get out of those old gacha machines from gas stations or pizza parlors). I have squishy foam fruits (if you haven't touched an iBloom fruit, please indulge yourself). I have a fidget cube, I have a beautiful egg-shaped makeup sponge, and I have a chewable from Stimtastic (sadly closed now).

I'm working on transferring the need to grind my teeth into squishing or squeezing things, and I'm working on trying to learn how to let myself unashamedly hand-flap. It's kind of stereotypical, sure, but have you ever done it? It's actually astounding how effective it is at burning out excess energy. And it's fun. If you're reading this, even if you're not autistic, I implore you to try it the next time you feel a bit overwhelmed. It doesn't have to be a full arm flap, you don't have to put a ton of power into it, but give it a try and see if you feel better after.

Even if you aren't autistic and don't quite understand the value of stimming, you've probably partaken without realizing. Have you ever been so excited that you bounced on your feet? Or have you ever been to a sporting event and gotten swept up in jumping, screaming, high-fiving, and fist-pumping? That is, technically, stimming. That's just experiencing a wealth of sensory or emotional information and physically expressing it, which is the core of autistic stimming.

I think my housemates especially enjoy it when I hand-flap because, usually, it denotes an overflow of joy. I very rarely instinctively do it when I'm upset or unhappy, it just explodes out of me when I'm excited or delighted by something. Now there's a feedback loop—I flap because I'm happy, my friends exclaim that I'm happy, and so I end up flapping more because...yeah! Yeah, I am happy!

The feeling is, honestly, incredibly freeing. I feel like I'm finally doing something that I've been supposed to be doing. It feels like a gulp of air after swimming underwater for just a moment too long.

It's shocking that as tactile as I am, I wasn't able to realize what kind of stims would suit me best until now, that my hands would be so important a tool not just for art and writing, but for recentering and improving my mood.

It's a running joke that when my family goes out to stores, anything that looks like it'll be a pleasing texture is pointed out to me. Testing soft pillows and blankets on display, sticking arms into clothing racks, squishing silicone cookware—these tasks have become part of the routine, everyone joining in and encouraging each other to partake.

That's not even touching on the delight I find in childish wares, the kind that we tend to try to discourage finding joy in as adults. I'll say it: I'm a total sucker for toys that are designed for pretend play. Fake kitchens with all those tiny utensils, and the fake food made of wood so it all clacks together so nicely. Those wonderfully squishy foam play mats that are shaped like puzzle pieces. At one point in the early 2000s, I owned every single Polly Pocket set that existed on the market, and it was all thanks to how sensorily pleasing all those tiny rubber clothing sets were.

And I'd do it again at 30. The squish and stretch was unmatched.

My newfound love for sensory-seeking behavior also persists in bookstores. I can't tell you the amount of funny looks I get from passersby when they get a glimpse of me opening a book to see what the pages smell like. Some books are just built different, okay? Sometimes they have that sweet, slightly acrid ink smell—sometimes you can almost tell what kind of wood the paper pulp was created from. If they're glossy, maybe they have that slick, specific manufactured smell that you can almost taste on the back of your tongue. Sometimes they're incredibly soft, like the paper that is typically used in Bibles, so feathery that it feels like just turning the page might crumple it beyond saving. And that's more than doubled in the journal section, where you're likely to find a ton of journals that are leather-bound. Is there any smell more comforting than a leather-bound journal? Any sensation more pleasing than the soft glide of high-quality leather under your fingers? The satisfying "fwhip" of the pages as you let them shuffle through your hand? I doubt it. It's the whole package.

As I write this, I wonder what this book is going to feel like. Is it going to have smooth pages, or those pulpier ones? Will the cover be slick or matte? Will it be bright, or pastel, or surprisingly neutral? How many stories like mine (or unlike mine!) are going to be preserved inside? All of us together, making an autistic chorus. Despite all my preferences, I can't find myself caring too terribly much about the little details. The most important part of the book will be all of the stories contained inside, all the voices of people I've never met but have this kinship with.

So often, being autistic can feel like you don't have much of a voice, or that your voice is wrong—too loud, too weird, too uncomfortable for everyone around you.

Not here though. Not now.

I can't wait to hold this book, and finally read the experiences of everyone else within its pages.

I can't wait to see all the different versions of autistic pride, bound in paper and ink and glue, a sort of tribute to all of us.

That, more than anything, is joy.

The Joy of Comedy

Charlie Lee George

A writer and stand-up comedian from Swindon, Charlie now lives in Margate and performs across the UK and abroad.

Trigger warning: child abuse.

I found out in my 30s during a global pandemic that I was on the autism spectrum.

Finding out I was neurodiverse later in life was like suddenly realizing that the reason you've been struggling all these years is that you've been speaking your own language. Turns out not everyone starts a conversation with: What's your exact salary?

A lot of people have said to me since I started sharing this realization publicly, "But you don't look autistic." To which I've replied, in what I now know to be my typically atypical way, "Well, you don't look ignorant...but you know, it's a spectrum."

Initially I was diagnosed with attention deficit hyperactivity disorder (ADHD) and put on stimulant medication, which did exactly what it said on the tin: made me incredibly overstimulated, so much so I started stimming, repeatedly pacing up and down and flapping my hands and arms to manage my racing thoughts, like Rocky Balboa in a classic movie training montage. Only the thing I was preparing to fight was myself, and a whole lot of overwhelming memories and puzzle pieces being revealed to me that I could never unsee.

A relative had recently been late-diagnosed with Asperger's syndrome, a term no longer recognized and replaced with autism spectrum disorder—though I much prefer the term "condition"! At a similar time, another relative had it confirmed that they were also autistic and were likely to need a lot of ongoing support. Suddenly traits of various other family members also began to align. My mother's struggles over many years. Observing my grandmother's strict patterns and routines at home that couldn't be broken. My father's struggle to emotionally connect, preferring to escape into science fiction and other worlds he had special interests in.

It was all becoming startlingly clear.

Could the reason I had struggled to "cope" all these years, kept longing to know why I wasn't able to sustain myself "like other people," and found things so difficult that "other people" found easy, be that I was not, as I had been told, "mentally ill," but that I had been trying constantly to manage and suppress the same condition as the rest of my diagnosed, and undiagnosed, family?

This sinking realization was like getting sucked under a big wave, then being pummeled over and over every time you try to stand back up. I think the shorthand for that process is called grief.

In preparation for my adult autism assessment I had to get back in touch with my mother, a woman I'd describe as a cross between Rab

C. Nesbitt and Hyacinth Bucket. A devout Jehovah's Witness and angry Scottish woman, fond of shouting about Jesus in a Laura Ashley dress.

My mother astounded me by having no disagreement whatsoever that there was, in her words, "definitely something seriously wrong with me," and that she had always suspected I'd had some sort of "brain damage." Had it been that time she'd looked away and I'd fallen off a swing and cracked my head open? Or various other mishaps in my unregulated council childhood playground? Or perhaps my "traumatic" birth with which she seemed to relish regaling anyone who would listen.

What she was able to clarify, somewhat embarrassingly, was that I had never been obsessed with trains, but instead always...girls. She recalled that my short-term memory was terrible but that I could recount facts about a girl I'd been obsessed with from years ago as if they had never left my mind.

She recounted my sarcastic and dry sense of humor, which was always too dark for her tastes, but she admired my ability to make fun of and laugh in the face of some of the worst circumstances, often finding humor in serious and ill-fated situations such as personal losses and failures.

She stated matter-of-factly that as a three-year-old, I had engaged in a full-scale imaginative world of my own making, complete with props and side characters, which no one was allowed to participate in.

That I regularly believed I was Atreyu from the 1980's film *The Neverending Story*, and had read the complete works of Shakespeare by eight years old.

I had obsessive routines, and would often be found sleeping in my school uniform so I wouldn't be late in the morning. Getting into heated debates with my teachers at school, I'd been described as an "old soul," who hated parties because I always had to be collected early because of my migraine headaches in reaction to the swirling lights and screaming children.

Also I would regularly wet myself at school, because I had taken the instructions to stand in line and not move too literally.

The evidence was beginning to stack up, and was compounded when she remembered that I insisted on being vegetarian as a child, when the rest of our household lived solely off spam and chicken Kievs, because of my "affinity with animals," which went as far as thinking I could communicate telepathically with them.

This fascination was exacerbated by the Jehovah's Witness literature that was heavily present in our lives at the time, featuring colorful images of lions and bears cuddling and playing in an everlasting paradise setting, with children and families laughing and smiling as the "former world" burnt to a crisp around them. This intense imagery led to me being bit by a squirrel, a swan, and a goat; the holy trinity of unfriendly animal encounters, and a valuable lesson that nature isn't always benevolent.

Getting affirmation that I was in fact autistic meant I could finally breathe out and stop searching for what was wrong with me. I had been desperately trying to contort to fit into the choke-hold myth of "normal."

Now I could just be me.

Only thing was, I didn't know remotely who I was at all.

* * *

I was really good at faking it growing up. I had to be, to fit the social conditions around me. I learnt how to smile wide, laugh loud, and give the impression that I was having a great time, when I don't think I even really knew what a good time was.

I knew I enjoyed reading in the dark in the cocoon of our airing cupboard, overidentifying with the central character in every story.

I enjoyed moving emphatically to music with my eyes closed. I suppose, looking back, this was stimming? A version of it at least. I had kept most stims under wraps, using more socially acceptable actions I could do repeatedly with my hands, like ordering things, twiddling my hair, or washing and moisturizing my hands. Nothing strange or peculiar about compulsions like this for a young girl.

I also enjoyed collecting things I was interested in or fascinated by: marbles, crystals, pebbles, kaleidoscopes, secret crushes on girls at school...but joy? Inside yourself? Or with others? I wouldn't know where to begin.

I think I was always more focused on survival, at least when it came to interacting with other people. I used to rehearse conversations ahead of time, studying others carefully and mimicking the interactions I thought you were supposed to have. I learnt that if you asked questions and kept the focus on the other person they would happily steer the conversation around to what was bothering them at the time, and you could avoid the embarrassment of having no real clue what was appropriate to talk about, or why you would want to talk with others you didn't know or like at all.

My mother, being a devout Jehovah's Witness, had trained my sister and I to speak eloquently to strangers early, via a religious script, as we went door to door near our hometown of Swindon, selling the idea of impending apocalypse and the promise of salvation in the Wiltshire countryside.

I owe her, as she was the catalyst and ammunition for what would later become one of the biggest sources of joy in my life. Comedy.

I don't think I could conceive of a better incongruity joke than the world coming to an apocalyptic end at an unspecified date and the promise of salvation in paradise, reserved only for a random 144,000 people. It was this type of perplexing and contradictory thought that would drive my obsession with taking things that made no sense to me and putting them together, pointing out the absurdity for a laugh.

As a child I started taking late 1990s and early 2000s advertising slogans, pairing them up with the ominous and prophetic imagery in Jehovah's Witnesses literature, *The Watchtower* and *Awake* magazines, and passing them around weekly Bible study, to see who I could get to crack and burst into hysterics before getting dragged out and punished. Looking back, these were my early attempts at jokes, and worth every beating from my mother.

This, and impressions. I used to do killer impressions of the types of characters we'd meet going door to door, re-enacting for my sister the horrors of our embarrassment by empowering ourselves to take the piss out of those who had rejected us. From neo-Nazis, to hoarders and Mormons, no one was spared the wrath of our bouffon clowning and mockery. If anyone was going to be denied entry to paradise...it would definitely be us.

My mother agreed with me and I ended up leaving home in my early teens after an explosive dispute about beliefs—I had developed a strong belief in evolution and getting off with girls—she wasn't a fan of either.

I don't think I realized how much my childhood had affected me until after I left, and all I seemed capable of doing in the big wide world was acting like a swan, presenting a graceful, high-achieving image of myself that would glide effortlessly across the surface, whilst paddling twice as fast beneath, covering all my autistic traits and challenges. Or, as it felt at the time, unconsciously keeping them out of view so as to avoid failure, rejection, or punishment. All that watching others, mimicking others, trying to be others, had meant I could pass successfully. But now I had to keep up the pretense of "fitting in."

I was like an undercover agent, passing for normal and a "good girl," but the person whose life I was destroying with my superpowers of suppression was in fact my own. I put my childish daydreaming and joke telling aside, in a desperate attempt to follow the steps and structures of life everyone else deemed "successful" seemed to be taking.

Well, almost. I attempted conventional jobs, schooling, and university, but could never sit still for long enough or understand the rules to get ahead in those environments, so ended up being expelled, fired, or unexpectedly leaving every "proper" job I had. Regularly known as "the weirdo of the office," my eccentricities and hyper-sensitive nervous system could never withstand a probationary period.

I tended to fare better in self-employment, where I could make my own rules, and in alternative educational settings like circus school, where as a teenager I did a BTECH course instead of A levels, rediscovering my love of comedy and getting to be imaginative and physical to my heart's content.

After this course ended I did not fare well managing the multiple priorities of being completely financially independent at 16 and working part-time jobs to survive and support my creative business ventures, which included setting up my own dance company at 19, very much keeping the poised swan alive for the following years.

All that suppression began to catch up with me, transforming on the inside into a demolitions expert. Exploding and melting down, physically and mentally, in private. Inevitably the parts of me I'd severed to survive returned to remind me that they still very much existed and were not happy about being ignored.

Desperately I hid years of struggle, transient homelessness, challenges with fitting into work and academia, repeated and relentless burnouts, patterns of self-neglect, and struggles in communication and my personal relationships.

I was projecting the great and powerful Oz to the outside world, yet behind the curtain I literally could not keep up with the song and dance I'd made about what I was capable of.

In truth I had never been a swan. I was always a flamingo flailing awkwardly on one leg.

Until it all came crashing down.

* * *

The process of unmasking, for me, has largely been about getting back in touch with the version of myself that was right there at the center, all along. Peeling back the layers that were covered over to protect from the harshness of my environment, and attempts to make my presence more palatable, manageable, and acceptable in order to survive. Over-striving for the love that was evading my more challenging parts.

But being autistic has always brought me back to seeking truth. There, I found that in order to move forward, I needed to kill "normal" and "perfect," so that I could live more true to myself.

Underneath all that pedaling and performing was the soft, sweet weirdo that I always was. I would need to let the facade of the swan fall away and allow myself to be the awkward, gangly, colorful flamingo I really am.

Embracing and accepting the quirks of who I am has given me back the key to finding my true joy. Many of my first loves as an autistic little girl have come back into my life at full volume and in vivid color.

I was always immersed in storytelling, world building and creating characters in my head; now I do that for a living in screenwriting and stand-up comedy. Comedy has allowed me to bring into awareness the aspects of myself that had previously been rejected, suppressed, or denied as flaws. Suddenly now, being a weirdo with inappropriate thoughts and expressions, seeing things others don't see, making strange and wonderful new connections and associations is not only funny, but celebrated. Pouring my obsessions onto the page or into a microphone has allowed me to connect with others in ways I never thought possible.

When I stand on stage, I'm able to communicate effectively to large groups of people, making them laugh with my special interests—be that my takes on queer relationships, or my quirky perception of things from my myriad of "failures to normal." I feel less alone. I feel seen, heard, and valued in ways I rarely get to feel in my daily life.

I also get to smash preconceptions of what a neurodivergent person is and can do. Many people have commented on social media that they have empathized with what I've spoken about or been through, whether it be queer identity, rejection from family members, leaving a religion, struggling with transient homelessness, and attempting to manage mental health with "self-care" in the absence of quality, affordable services, and being true to yourself in the modern world.

My creativity, which was a form of escapism when I was young, has become a way for me to both understand the world and make a living. I now work full time as a self-employed stand-up comedian and writer and have an access support worker alongside me, to help me manage my challenges in the workplace. I no longer have to struggle alone anymore. We work together on tools and strategies that help me cope better with everyday life, supporting me through meltdowns and regulation.

I probably feel the most joy at how stand-up brings me back to my senses and the present moment, the place where I feel truly alive. When you're doing stand-up there's no time to worry about your obsessive to-do lists or any demands on you. It forces you to surrender to being right there in that space, with those people, interacting and connecting in a way with clearly defined rules—bar the odd heckler. We follow the rule that the speaker gets a set agreed time slot for their voice and material. This structure provides a sacred spotlit circle and a place for me to interact and engage with groups successfully, on my terms, leaving me feeling empowered and affirmed through the response of (hopefully!) laughter. I can receive positive feedback socially in a large group setting that I rarely get otherwise. I often leave carrying a sense of renewed belonging that ruptures the isolation that can come with being neurodivergent.

Having a job that involves travel has opened up the world to me and helped me embrace the dark; my favorite time of day. There's no better feeling than my post-gig night walks home, where I really get to shine, as finally the world is at last on the right setting for me. It's quiet. There's more space to think, feel, breathe, and process without all that overwhelming sensory input. Creative ideas can take flight in this special liminal time where I can really tune in to the environment, without so much noise and distortion.

When I arrive home at the train station near where I live in Margate in Kent, the lighting is low. Giant purple, red and white neon orb-like street lamps pave the way down the promenade. Not blaring, just illuminating the glisten of the tide as it rolls gently back and forth, the lapping waves scoring my walk home.

The moon beams down on the clock tower and I look up at what feels like an endless sky of perfectly designed mood lighting stars.

I watch a nearby dog zig-zag humorously along the pavement in front of me, scavenging for remnants of revelers' late-night takeaway chips.

As I reflect on what I achieved, or didn't, I begin to unfurl now, leaving all activity and expectation behind, tuning in to my heightened senses, but just for me.

I let my ears flood with the sounds of my favorite playlist of "songs I'm obsessed with," over 200 songs of varying genres that I listen to on repeat, finding new details in them each time. Songs of power, songs for crying, songs with words that evoke memories or laughter, songs with drums that follow the rhythm of my heartbeat.

Maybe, just maybe, here in these quiet moments, when I am not anybody's—not a performer, a partner, a daughter, or an autistic woman struggling to fit the world—I can feel safe enough under the cover of darkness to just let it all fall down. To let my arms float up, flap, and glide like aeroplane wings under the night sky, stimming to my heart's content. To my own private revolutionary offbeat.

The Joy of Repetition

Laura Kate Dale

In the year 2022, I listened to the song The Foundations of Decay by My Chemical Romance over 400 times, according to a popular streaming service that tracks such information. I know that number is inaccurate, as it didn't track the times I listened to it on YouTube, or as part of a mix I made for myself to listen to when swimming.

The song also didn't come out until May of that year, meaning that number only accounts for a little over half of a calendar year.

The song is six minutes long. Just counting the 400 times I have a number for, that means I spent 40 hours during that year listening to a single song, often multiple times back to back.

The thing is, for me, this is not unusual, but a pretty accurate reflection of how I interact with not just music, but video games, TV shows, and even foods. I am a creature of repetition, and there's no way I would rather be.

For many people, repetition is not a particularly enjoyable experience. Maybe you'll watch a favorite movie once every couple of years, or listen to a favorite artist's discography whenever you're in the car, but most people do not latch onto specific singular experiences and truly immerse themselves in them.

As an autistic person, repetition is pure joy to me.

Now, as to why I enjoy repetition so much, some answers are more obvious, and some are more abstract. Some are diagnostically observed, and some are more nebulous and personal.

For the basics, repetition is predictability. If I have experienced a piece of media before, I know what's going to happen, and am not going to be caught off guard by a subversion of expectations that causes me anxiety or distress. If I eat a meal I have eaten before, prepared identically, I can rely on not being caught unaware by a rogue flavor or texture combo that my body might reject. I can relax, knowing what is coming.

If you asked a clinician to explain my repetitive behaviors, this is probably what they would point to.

But, for me, repetition is much more often about indulgence, appreciation, and discovery. It's about taking something I know well, and finding something new in it. It's about appreciating a part I had not appreciated before, or a new understanding of why I enjoy the things I enjoy, and getting beyond the surface level of the things that bring me joy.

Where, for many, repeated exposure leads to diminishing returns, for me the opposite is true. The more I listen to that song, the more I can follow it precisely in my mind throughout. I am not trying to learn the basics, I am freed up to explore what else makes up the piece of art. I have the space mentally to pull apart the threads of the work, and see how it is assembled. I am able to sing along, knowing every word and inflection, having taken the time to really understand what is being conveyed, and feel it alongside the movements of the song. As someone who struggles to follow unstated subtext in real time, repeated listens of a song, or viewings of a movie, can give me more of a chance to pick up on meaning others might find comes more naturally. Picking out a single song lyric, and really listening to how it fits into the wider piece of music, can make my appreciation of the track better as a whole.

My repetitions don't tend to last forever; they eventually cycle, but they last for long enough. They often last for months, and months, and months, eventually passing, but always returning with time. Which song I am playing on loop may change, as may the comfort meal I prepare for myself each day, but there's always something my brain that decides what it wants to really get to know as well as it can.

I could bounce from song, to song, to song. Instead, I pick one, and I bury myself within it, seeing what there is to find when you know something down to its core.

Let's Build a Nest Together

Liia Alice M.

As an autistic person, I've always felt weirdly connected with octopuses. Interestingly enough I am not the only one to have made this connection: while considering how to start this essay, I googled "octopus autism," and found multiple texts in which other people parallel their autism to the behavior of octopuses.

One of the essays I read detailed the way octopuses developed intelligence, despite being mostly antisocial, proving the former theory about intelligence evolving due to social needs for communication, bonding, and establishing hierarchies at the very least incomplete.

Just like the octopus developed intelligence without social pressure, autistic people experience the richness of intelligence, even though we often have difficulty reading social cues and tend to be oblivious to social hierarchies.

Compared to many other invertebrates, the lack of a shell is a defining feature of the octopus. It made the octopus vulnerable, but also forced them to advance other means of survival.[1] Similarly to

1 Carolyn Gage (2020) Ruminations on octopuses and autism. Accessed October 11, 2022 at https://carolyngage.weebly.com/blog/ruminations-on-octopuses-and-autism

the octopus evolving their incredible camouflage, we autistic people create our own safety tools out of necessity.

While I see many other aspects of my behavior reflected in octopuses—their playful nature, how they reach out with their arms to explore their surroundings, the affectionate bonds they form with some other octopuses even though often they prefer to be alone—I want to focus on one behavior in particular: nesting.

Many animals build nests. For most of them it's part of their reproductive cycle. Birds build their nests, lay eggs, hatch them, and raise their babies until they are independent enough to leave the nest. Octopuses are different; while often more temporary, they build nests even when they don't intend to lay or hatch eggs.

Perhaps you have seen a video—if you had the honor to see it in person instead, I envy you—of an octopus holding onto human junk, like bottles, pipes, or cups, before squishing themselves inside. It doesn't seem like they do this only to hide and shelter themselves. They're selective; yes, often they use literal trash, but they don't use just any trash but only the best they can find. They seek to build something more, something that gives them a place to huddle in, comfort, a home.

I am like the octopus; while I've never reproduced, I build nests regularly. Usually that includes neither sticks and branches, nor the kind of things we dispose of in the sea, but the most comfortable and fluffy stuff my apartment has to offer—blankets, pillows, and my girlfriend.

When I first started nesting—perhaps I was around eight—it looked quite unlike it does today. Primarily it was a way to tell stories, and imagine other worlds.

Maybe I and the blankets piled around me would represent a castle that was under siege. I'd spot the enemy's troops coming from the other side of the room, prepare my fort as well as possible, strategize and send my warriors—either my Playmobil figures or my plushies—into combat.

Maybe my nest would be a secluded farm that needed to sustain itself. My plushies would be the livestock, and yet together we'd cultivate the fields. Over time we'd expand our land, grow all kinds of crops, and build new sheds.

Maybe—no, honestly, mostly it was the siege story. This was around the time I was watching a lot of *Lord of the Rings*, and the battle of Helm's Deep was apparently weighing heavy on me.

Growing up in a loving but not necessarily understanding environment, and slowly aging beyond the time play is endorsed, I stopped nesting for many years.

Nesting is intimate; it's an emotional release, it's cathartic. Therefore it was something that I did when I was alone, and yet, the shame and embarrassment moved me to mask my playful self. Only when a former partner of mine showed me that I was allowed to be myself—however quirky that might be—did I pick up this activity again. I rediscovered nesting as a tool to escape the unintelligible world I am surrounded with, manually building the shell that I, just like the octopus, never had.

When surrounded by blankets and pillows—one to each side of you—the world suddenly becomes so much more quiet, and its horrors more bearable. My skin is easily pierced, it's such a vulnerable barrier between myself and the world. Constructing a thicker layer of protection gives me the feeling of security that I crave. Though the word "security" is not strong enough; in German we'd call it Geborgenheit. A word that symbolizes safety, protection, and invulnerability on one side, but also a being at peace with yourself and the world, a warm closeness where you intuitively know that it's safe to sleep.

But let's go back a step. You may be asking, "How exactly does it look to build a nest?" or "Can I build a nest myself?" To another person, nesting may mean something entirely different than it does to me, or an octopus.

A friend of mine describes herself as nesting when she gets overwhelmed by excitement about the space she lives in, and starts to clean up and improve her apartment, creating more of herself within it step by step. But let me take you on the journey of how I nest. And if you'd like, you're welcome to join in.

It starts with a good foundation, something you want to snuggle yourself into: let's take the bed as an example. Almost any emotion—happiness, overextension, excitement, or boredom—can act as a catalyst. Usually the bed already contains a few pillows and one or two blankets, though well-prepared beds will obviously keep more than that on hand. Perfect conditions to start with.

Personally I like to wrap my weighted blanket around my legs—especially when I nest to get rest. It helps me air out all of the bad emotions inside of me and soothes me. It gives my senses a new sensation to focus on, one that is stable and immovable, easy to navigate and process. This anchor is what I will use to create new feelings.

What's next should feel wonderful to all those who—like me—relate to goblins and dragons. Stretch as wide as you can and, with your arms far out, reach for all the blankets and pull them towards you. While you stretch, try to feel your muscles tensing, so that you can feel the release of pulling everything close even more intensely. And, although it is not yet a nest, it becomes a hoard—a hoard of your future comfiness.

Now let us transform the blanket pile into a proper nest. Search the hoard for the things you want to build into your wall. Pillows make for a great foundation that can be extended with blankets. Place them around your body; I like my nest to be minimal, to feel like everything is within reach and within my control. All my walls will be in direct contact with myself, the nest as an extension of my body—my shell. If you think that it won't overwhelm you, let yourself constantly feel the softness of the blocks you build with. Let the pillows and blankets slide over your skin before you squish them into the correct form, and place them where they belong. Don't be afraid to restructure the parts you're unhappy with, again and again.

An essential part of the nest that many may forget about is the ceiling. There are a few different ways to build your ceiling. I like to just pull a blanket over my head until I am in complete darkness. While my arms keep dragging the blanket over me and I feel the friction of the fabric on my hair, I push my head slightly forward, bursting out at the other end of the blanket with my face like a kangaroo out of its mother's pouch. My hands still on the blanket, I pull them together so that it leaves a small hole for my head, and maybe my arms, like a hoodie. This is especially comfy on a rainy autumn day with a hot chocolate.

With a blanket large enough, this ceiling is easily transformable. It can cover your shoulders or head, but pulling it over your face and down to stuff it underneath the outer walls of your nest gives you complete protection against anything outside in an instant. Quickly throwing a blanket over everything is a perfectly fine way to create a ceiling as well.

When I want my nest to be filled by darkness though, so that I can shut off my sight entirely, I will first lay the blanket which will become the ceiling on top of the nest and myself, then stretch my arms between the new ceiling and the outer walls to grab the edge of the blanket, and wrap it around the bottom of the wall from the outside.

Not only does this provide darkness, the act itself—the stuffing around the whole nest—is an effortful experience, one that makes it tangible, how bit by bit you make sure that your future self will be in the darkness and isolation you desire. Not only is it alleviating to remove the impressions of sight for a while, it also offers an empty canvas for daydreaming.

Please never forget an air vent in your construction. Usually I take part of the ceiling and roll it in so that it leaves a small hole between the walls and the ceiling. The doubled-up blanket that is created in this way is surprisingly stable. If you want your nest to be as dark as possible, you can do that in a place that doesn't directly interfere with your vision. Sometimes it becomes difficult to breathe nonetheless, and I have to open up my ceiling.

And that's it all ready: a nest. If you've followed along—maybe it is your first—I hope you can find the same comfort and joy in yours as I find in mine. Of course there are many things you can personalize about it and the process to get there.

My nest becomes my retreat, my hideout, a place I can be myself no matter what is going on around me. I can use it to escape my responsibilities—even if it's just for a moment. Nothing save myself can remind me of them. I can distract myself with something I enjoy, reading or watching a show, or I might get sucked into more nest building. When the latter happens, I become all excited about the warmth and comfort my current nest gives and want to reach out with it. Getting lost in the sensory joy of feeling the components in my hand, feeling them brushing against me and coming together, I seek to extend that joy and rebuild, improve, or wallow in it.

To expand the nest further, the materials provided by the bed itself usually aren't enough. You can grab anything that looks soft enough to restock. Oh, also if you want any plushies in your nest, better get them now. Very common company in my nests is our meter-long BLÅHAJ shark Stella, who makes for a great isolation on the side or just a piece to wrap myself around completely while in the nest, as well as members of the Dynosty—our four mighty queer dinosaurs, each with their own royal title: the three tyrannosauruses Rex, Allure, and Saia, and their ankylosaurus mount Lacquosho. Just like many autistic peers who commonly attribute human characteristics to non-human objects,[2] I revel in talking with my dinosaurs and imagining their thoughts and ideas. Today my plushies are guests—or part of the construction. But, unlike in my childhood, they don't need to give their lives for me anymore.

Once I acquire the material, I just throw it onto the current nest. Yes, often that will destroy the creation—and if it doesn't, the next step will—but I am overflowing with excitement, I don't care that I have to rebuild. Usually I will express my excitement by just straight-up diving into the bed, often pulling my girlfriend behind me. After burrowing myself to the bottom of the soft pyramid, I will just sit there for a bit,

2 Rebekah C. White & Anna Remington (2019) Object personification in autism: This paper will be very sad if you don't read it, *Autism* 23(4), 1042–1045.

letting all the impressions flow through me, purring a bit like a kitten who can't get enough of her belly rubs. It is this ability to reliably rush my whole body with joy or relaxation by submerging myself in the nest that makes this the experience I want to write about.

Flooded by energy and euphoria, I jump, and giggle, and start rubbing my face all over the blanket, once again like a kitten marking her territory.

Randomly grabbing some of the blankets around me, feeling their malleability and arranging them to my liking, slowly I lose myself in the process. It is a moment of pure freedom and joy. Rarely is there another opportunity in my life where I can allow emotions to become so intense, and let them accumulate over time without having to worry about them becoming overwhelming.

Constantly building, expanding, rebuilding, tearing parts down, and starting anew. Believe me that—especially with a weighted blanket—the process is very exhausting after a while. But it's a wonderfully rewarding kind of exhausting. It's like when you come back from a ten-kilometer run. You struggle to catch up with your breathing and your legs are burning, but you know: I did that, and I can be so proud of myself.

Eventually the exhaustion leaves and is replaced by calm. Curled up around Stella, I will follow the newest chapter of my favorite webcomics, or delve into the depths of the internet to find the newest—or oldest—undiscovered lesbian stories. Inside the coziness of my nest, I dare to explore emotions which would be overwhelming if I risked feeling them in the open.

While a nest is all about its inside, the outside doesn't cease to exist.

And so, the nest can be used to interact with the world: it can be used to hide yourself in, but also to invite another person nearby, and to show them your emotions from a position of safety.

If I am completely hidden within my nest, no part of my body extending beyond its reach, it signals that the world, and maybe also the presence of the other person, is too much for me. It gently asks them to give me space for myself. I feel less vulnerable knowing they respect that physical manifestation of my boundaries, so they will respect the less tangible ones as well.

Often though, I'll continuously peek out, just pulling away enough blanket so I can observe them with one eye, and quickly retreat once they look back. This will initiate communication between us. Most likely they are curious what it's about. Maybe I am embarrassed about something and don't dare to tell them myself, or there is something important that I want to—or need to—talk about but don't know how to express.

Not seeing my conversation partner's reaction makes it easier to not overinterpret it; to not think the wrinkle in their lips displays their disdain, to not think the disagreement apparent on their face is an evaluation of myself. It may be easier if the other person plays twenty questions, and you only need to say yes or no. You could even declare the nest neutral grounds, where you can try out words you wouldn't say otherwise and thoughts that aren't quite manifested yet, and explore a side of you that you don't usually show to people because you're worried they might judge you.

Being surrounded by the nest gives me a feeling of cuteness. It is easier to assume good faith in others when you're cute yourself, and easier to expect softness—because that's how people commonly react to cuteness. It also gives a certain self-worth that allows you to ask for accommodations that you otherwise often feel undeserving of.

Over time, nesting has become one of the most important and easiest tools of communication in my relationship; it allows me to overcome the vulnerability that I feel while communicating with others.

Nesting is a behavior that involves, and facilitates, unmasking a lot of my autistic traits. I have to feel safe engaging with sensory exploration to build the nest, and often unmask other behaviors once inside. Therefore nesting when I am not alone, inviting someone else into my nest, or even building the nest together with them, is a sign of trust. As such it also becomes a sign of love. The nest at times may be the physical manifestation of the relationship and a place to celebrate said love. It can offer the room to experience joy in a multitude of ways together.

Once the exhilaration of nest building and being inside the nest fades, I slowly turn to different activities. As I've already written, it often leads to reading or cuddling. My body relaxes from its huddled-together position into a more stretched-out form, turning the nest itself back into pillows and blankets. They are still warm and continue to provide comfort. With time some of the blankets, and especially the plushies—I am so sorry—land on the ground around the bed. Eventually I will put all the blankets and pillows back where they came from. While it hurts a bit to get them out of the bed, I know that my girlfriend will keep complaining that our bed is too full and that there isn't enough space for her if I keep all of them. Another day the cycle will start again.

Contentment in Chaos

Alex Hill

Queer AutDHD writer, activist, and joy-bringer
living with two partners in North East UK.

My position is one of contentment in chaos. The lights are bright and the cooker fan is whirring. The hiss of a frying pan sends sound, heat, and savory scent into the air. I'm in the corner, away from the worst of the turmoil, sitting in a swinging egg chair. It's been designed for use outside, but who's to say where it should go, really? It's comfy, the high sides surrounding me like a little cocoon of safety in a stimulating environment, and the rocking motion provides a soothing sensation. I've decorated it by weaving faux flower stems and little succulents into the outside. It is a place so perfect and so mine.

This story is about finding joy even in everyday vulnerable or difficult places, armed with the knowledge that I am autistic. This story is about how my neurodiverse family has changed and adapted to ensure I have the time and space—both physical and mental—to flourish and thrive. This story is about understanding myself, giving and receiving care, and the joy that comes from this.

Mine is a queer, polyamorous household with intersecting disabilities, so the way we give and receive care is often drastically different from cultural norms. While queer sexuality and neurodiversity are not inherently linked, statistics suggest that these traits overlap more often than expected, and that's certainly true of my family. Personally, I've always had an inclination towards questioning societal norms, which led me to discover and thrive in polyamorous relationships. I live with two long-term partners, Jasper and Harriet, giving and receiving love and care in radical and completely made-up ways. In terms of their brains, Harriet was recently diagnosed with ADHD and while Jasper doesn't feel a particular connection to ADHD or autism, he is a very neurodiverse-compatible human whose brain gels well with mine. With a range of neurotypes represented in our household, we can use our complementary aspects to care for each other and create the best home for ourselves.

One aspect of this care for me is reliability. For me and many other autistic people, unpredictability can make the world a confusing and hostile place, but reliability can act as a counterbalance to make things a little easier. There are a lot of small ways, day to day, that my partners and I add routine and predictability to my life, and while they might sound insignificant to other people, they mean the world to me. One example of this is that whenever my partners bring me a cup of squash, they use the same cup every time and weigh the amount of juice that goes in the bottom.

I found out that Harriet had started weighing the juice when she began asking me if the squash was too strong or too weak. Usually when I'm asked if a drink is okay, I'll say that of course it's lovely. I don't want to make a fuss! To get around this social reflex, Harriet asked me questions that were more like: "If you had to say if the juice was too strong or too weak, what would you say?" That was a much easier question to answer because there aren't any social expectations wrapped up in it. Gradually, she calibrated the juice to my preference. It was only when we got towards the end of the process and she started pressing me on whether it was too strong or too weak that I found out she was trying to get the amount exactly right to the gram.

When I asked Harriet why she was weighing it, she told me that she had noticed that when the juice was too strong or too weak, I would taste it and look disappointed. There's a stereotype that autistic people are generally very closed off with their emotions, but I've always been the opposite. I've always worn my heart on my sleeve, my face betraying things that I didn't know I was feeling. Harriet told me that if the juice wasn't right, I would often just leave it on the side, forget about it, and then later wonder why I was still thirsty.

Hearing this was very difficult at first—was I picky or rude or ungrateful? Harriet reassured me that this wasn't the case, but it was hard to shake the feeling that this precision wasn't something that "normal" people would want, wasn't something that I should want. I felt guilty that she was doing this extra step for me. Surely it was much too much of a hassle for Harriet to weigh it when it tastes basically the same if you measure it by eye? But evidently, according to my body, it wasn't the same.

Not realizing I was autistic meant it was hard to understand why I wouldn't drink imperfect juice. Now that I understand myself better, I know that taste is just another one of my senses that is sensitive, and that's okay. Asking for my juice to be made the same going forward then felt much more reasonable and easier to accept. Now I feel so loved and accepted for who I am whenever I drink juice, knowing that it has been measured as an act of care by one of my loved ones. And it contributes to the reliability in my life; instead of being buffeted by a million things that are a little bit wrong, it's now a million minus one things.

Many marginalized people find it difficult to get an "official" diagnosis of autism, and I am no exception. It was a friend of a friend who initially asked me if I had ever thought I might be autistic when I was 24. That question firmly planted roots and I began to research autism—not just the symptoms as they appear to other people, but what it felt like to be autistic.

Oh, I don't like the big light being on? Maybe I'm sensitive to light, like autistic people. Oh, I find ambulance sirens more distressing than most people? That's how autistic people experience them too. Sometimes I get so overwhelmed that I feel like I can't talk or move? Huh, maybe that's not depression but autistic shutdown. By the time it came to my official autism assessment, my partners and I were convinced that I was autistic.

It's one thing to know that marginalized people are underdiagnosed with autism, but it was quite another to be faced with that reality for myself. Although there are various routes to diagnosis, the test that I was given had been developed for children five years of age and under. I could easily put together a jigsaw, understand common metaphors I had memorized the meanings of, and tell the assessors what emotions felt like. I was completely blindsided when the assessors, neither of whom were doctors, told me that they would not diagnose me due to those test results, despite how well my symptoms and history fit the diagnostic criteria. Since then I have been informally diagnosed by a doctor, but I would have to pay £900 to make this official, ultimately to have a label for what I already know about myself. Official diagnosis or not, it doesn't change how I experience the world, which is in an undeniably autistic way.

After the results of the assessment, I felt by turns doubtful of my self-knowledge, and misunderstood by the assessors. But I had waited a year for the assessment, and the knowledge I had built up about how I interact with the world was still there inside me and refused to be dismissed by a couple of strangers and some tick-boxes. Many autistic people gain confidence after receiving a medical diagnosis, but I managed to find it even after being refused one.

I vividly remember waking up a couple of days after the assessment filled with a new determination to explore more ways of making my life more joyful, official diagnosis be damned.

One place we found fertile ground to explore was the kitchen. My autistic brain struggles to tune out any kind of sensory input. Take a moment to imagine the various sights, sounds, smells, tastes, and textures that you experience whilst cooking. For me, it's like having to focus on all of those things at once. This makes the kitchen an overwhelming environment, even if I'm not doing the cooking. Just experiencing this barrage of sensations at the end of the day can drain my energy completely. Once we understood that being in the same room as someone else cooking was energetically expensive for me, we became able to manage it. If I started to feel overwhelmed, most often manifesting as a feeling of sadness or fatigue, I could simply leave the room.

Instead of fighting against the daily dinner drill, I try to embrace this time. I acknowledge that it's a great time for a rest when I'm low on energy and the sensory input is about to get a lot more intense. With practice, I usually manage my energy levels well enough that I can be in the kitchen with whoever is cooking, supporting them socially and mentally throughout the process. But I also try to allow myself to step away from the situation if I need to, though this is an ongoing battle against internalized ableism and is not easy! In these circumstances, I'll actively go and make a comfortable, low-sensory environment and rest, or do small activities until I can replenish my energy with food.

In our household with different neuro-perspectives, just my presence in the kitchen when able supports the cooking process and makes our lives run much more smoothly. After work, Jasper is often in need of social contact, so being in the kitchen with him makes cooking a much more fun activity. It's a chance for us to connect, talk and joke around. I'll also listen to him talk about his day, providing some much-needed emotional support. At the same time, I monitor which ingredients he's using up and make sure to add them to our shared shopping list, so that we're much less likely to run out of something unexpectedly. This means that food is more reliably available, providing another counterbalance to the chaos of the world.

For Harriet, my presence in the kitchen is even more important. First, her ADHD brain thrives with other people to bounce off. Even if I'm in the room doing something else, my mere presence helps her to get started. This is a technique from the ADHD community known as body doubling. We do it whenever there is work to be done, in all kinds of situations, be it cooking, or writing a report for her day job. Harriet benefits from being told the steps in the recipe in order, one at a time. The way her brain works, it is extremely difficult for her to break from the flow of cooking to check the recipe and process what to do next. It's also hard for her to remember more than one step at a time. It brings me such satisfaction to be able to help her so easily by just telling her what to do next. Similar to her weighing the juice for me, it's easy for one of us to do and helps the other a disproportionate amount. Understanding the bi-directional nature of our caring relationship has helped me realize how much she gets out of looking after me, and in turn helped me ditch my guilt in favor of happiness in caring and being cared for.

In this way, our neurodiversities complement each other and allow us to function beautifully as a unit. The way that we share kitchen tasks allows each of us to take on the jobs we are good at and lean on others when we would struggle alone. The things that I do to enable all of us to eat, from doing a weekly shopping order and thinking about what to have for dinner (taking into account everyone's schedules and capacity for cooking), to my physical presence and help in the kitchen, make me feel like I'm nurturing a smoothly functioning family unit. We have each learned to accept support from each other and are thriving as individuals as a result. Being able to use my strengths as an autistic person to enable my family to flourish, and being able to rely on them for help in turn, makes me positively tingle with joy.

Finding out how we can support each other's neurodiversities is an ongoing experiment in our household. I have lived most of my life masking my autism. Having hidden or ignored my feelings for so long, it is difficult to work out what I actually need on a day-to-day basis. Exploring how we can better care for each other, whether it's by measuring juice or reading out a recipe, is therefore a process of trial and error. The joy I feel when we discover something that helps is immense, whether I'm giving or receiving care, and brings with it a reinforced feeling of connection to my loved ones.

Autistic people have a unique relationship with their sensory environment which is usually portrayed as negative, but for me there is a flip side to that coin. Neurotypical people don't seem to experience the same delight that I do when feeling a soft texture, or putting the back of a cold teaspoon to my lips, or watching raindrops run down a window. Not knowing that I was autistic for so long meant that I didn't have much practice in seeking autistic sensory joy. My everyday experience has become much better since realizing that as well as mitigating negative sensations, we can also include more pleasant ones in our lives.

Take, for example, my recent birthday. Not only did the presents I received bring me joy in themselves, but they engaged my autistic sensory delight and left me feeling so thoroughly understood and loved. Jasper bought me a super soft plaid shirt, which I have hardly taken off since. It has poppers instead of buttons and I love the sound and feel of them as they pop on and off. It was from the "men's" section—I enjoy that my autism helps me to see past binary gender norms. Instead of gender categories, my category is softness or comfort or delight.

For her part, Harriet bought me a lava lamp, which is a lovely visual stim. Allowing myself to accept it as a stimulus to be enjoyed means that I can consciously watch it to relax, welcoming in the calm. We have also put it on a timer switch so that it's always warmed up in time for bed and it never stays on too long. This regularity helps a lot in setting up for bedtime, another area I have struggled with in the past.

Before I talk about how we have improved the sensory environment for sleep, I have to credit melatonin's amazing stabilizing effect on my sleep cycle. The hormone melatonin is produced in the body and tells you when to go to sleep, but for me and some other autistic people, our bodies seem not to create enough. I spent years talking about sleep hygiene with medical professionals but no matter how hard I tried, I couldn't break the cycle of not being able to sleep one day and then only being able to sleep the following night because I was utterly exhausted. Being on melatonin supplements has completely changed my life, not only in terms of improved sleep, but also in turn improving my overall mood and ability to cope with sensory input.

Having improved my biological relationship with sleep, my family and I started to build joy into my bedtime routine, particularly with regard to sensation. I can't begin to wind down with a strong light on so low lighting is key for me before I even start going to bed. To facilitate this, Jasper bought some Wi-Fi plugs so that we can turn the lamps on and off with our phones, making it much easier to transition smoothly to lower lighting. We use a yummy lavender spray to give the bedroom a calming smell. My favorite nights are when Jasper goes into the bedroom before me and sprays it; when I open the door and the scent is already in the air it feels like magic. Harriet started buying bamboo bedding because the softness of the texture is fabulous and its temperature-regulating properties help me to stay at the right temperature all night. I try to keep my bedroom cooler than the rest of the house so that I can snuggle down into the softness of the blankets, and I build a nest out of pillows and stuffed toys, which keeps my body in a comfortable position overnight.

Ending each day ensconced in the sensory joy of my bedroom has at last begun to feel like a good thing. I finally understand how sanctuary feels instead of just knowing what the word means. In the same way that recognizing that I'm autistic has improved so many other aspects of my life, it has been the key to a peaceful bedtime experience, allowing us to manipulate the sensory environment for pleasure as well as managing discomfort. Now I love to calm my mind and fall into a gentle sleep listening to the voices of my loves tell the same familiar stories over and over again, and I don't mind that that seems weird. Knowing that I'm autistic has brought me not only contentment in chaos but also in peace.

Learning It Was Okay to Be Nonverbal

Laura Kate Dale

For a person who has made a career out of writing and speaking, words haven't always come naturally to me.

As a child with at the time undiagnosed autism, a lot of pressure was placed on me by the adults in my life to fit a mold of normalcy growing up. I was a naturally insular child, but I had a wide verbal vocabulary from a young age, which to many in my life looked like I was capable of communication, and therefore exaggerating any desire not to engage with others socially. I could talk at length when I was excited about a niche topic I was fixated on, so in my parents' eyes there was no reason I couldn't come down and make small talk at family gatherings with large numbers of guests.

I know there was no malice behind my parents' choice to push me toward verbal and social communication. There was a belief that if I was put into social situations, situations I found difficult, I could push through to the other side, and be a more adjusted adult as a result. It was basically teaching me to mask, to put up a facade of normalcy until I had the privacy to let it slip.

However, even looking back to my childhood, verbal communication was always a very calculated and deliberate act for me. It was an architectural process, and a means to an end.

When I had an obsessive hyperfixation, an interest I deeply wanted to absorb information on, verbal communication was a means to express my excitement. I had thoughts, and I wanted to share them in as much detail as I could in the hopes that someone would mirror my experiences and I would form a connection. Each word was chosen precisely, with the aim of finding someone who would understand what was important to me, and why.

Beyond that, verbal communication was a survival tool, and one filled with pitfalls.

Spoken English, on its surface, appears to be a very structurally logical language, where words have meanings, and their order follows understood principles. The problem is, words often have multiple meanings, unstated meanings, and implied meanings. The way you say a word, the words you emphasize, and the context of when you chime in with those words all change how they are perceived, and simple sentences can have catastrophic consequences if delivered incorrectly.

Often, someone will ask you how you are, then be upset or annoyed when you provide an honest answer, because they didn't actually expect more than a rehearsed platitude. If a question was not rhetorical and you assume it was, you come across as ignoring the speaker. Every conversation is a guessing game, which requires careful navigation.

As a child, I even wrote out physical flow charts to help me navigate rules as I discovered them, forming routes through conversations unscathed.

I had a childhood where I was very much pressured to be social, to take part in verbal conversations, and one where speaking was a sign you were engaged in those around you. This provided useful skills, but it also put a pressure on me to think that I was failing if I ever put verbal language to the side.

As an adult, I went into a very verbal career path. I'd put enough of my time over the years into studying how to safely navigate language that I could construct sensible sentences, and had enough pent-up hyperfixations to give me plenty of material to speak and write about.

I had practiced speech as a skill, and ultimately it was something I dedicated my life to. I made a career out of solidifying concepts into words of many forms.

Learning to let go of verbal speech sometimes was a difficult, but rewarding, journey.

In my 20s, I started dating Jane, a fellow autistic woman who would one day become my wife. She was sweet, funny, creative, and a big part of me feeling safe enough to take time, and space to start to unmask, and to explore what parts of myself felt comfortable, and which parts I needed occasional respite from.

I used to think that if I was in a social situation and conversation grew quiet, I was supposed to find something to fill the gap with. If everyone is quiet, people are having a bad time, and so you should keep the discussion going. Sitting in silence is being antisocial, and that's a failure of conversation.

Around Jane, things were different. Not straight away, it took some time, but gradually I started giving myself permission to sit in silence, and not feel guilty or paranoid that I was solely at fault for that.

Silence free from guilt helped me to see it wasn't such a scary thing.

The second step when it came to feeling more comfortable with nonverbal spells was echolalia, the repetition of sounds common to many autistic people. I realized that a small meow, more affirmation of existence than directed in meaning, was often easier for me than navigating small talk. If I just wanted my wife to know I was thinking of her, and not ignoring her presence, but didn't have any words to say, a small noise rather than a word was easier for me to communicate.

Then came the realization that I had already had spells of being nonverbal, even if I had not recognized them at the time. Often when going through a sensory meltdown, or agitated by changes in routine, one of the first things I tend to lose is my ability to form verbal speech. I find myself struggling to verbalize words, finding them easier to type, then also finding typing them difficult too. This was a source of conflict growing up—my going silent when stressed and most needing to explain my actions. It was already something I was predisposed to.

Then, it became about giving myself deliberate and knowing space for time spent nonverbal, from Twitch streams where I play video games as a virtual Ditto rather than being on camera, so there's no expectation of me talking out loud, to having conversations with my wife about the fact that my comfort with verbal speech fluctuates with my stress levels, and it started to become clearer.

Sometimes I need to let myself put verbal speech aside. It has for my whole life been a deliberate act of calculated craft, and that degree of careful selection and positioning of words doesn't come without a toll.

I can love the craft of speaking and writing, while also acknowledging that sometimes I need to give myself permission to set that obligation aside. Living with someone else who is autistic was vital for me, as otherwise I doubt I would ever have given myself that permission to opt out of having to use words to get through a tough day.

Sometimes it's okay to recognize that words have weight, pressure, and obligation.

Sometimes it's okay to recognize that words feel like they need handling with attention and care.

Sometimes, it's okay to put those weights aside, and take a break from all of the obligations that verbal speech tends to come packaged alongside.

Post

Robin Wu

Nottingham-based 30-year-old cat lover,
headbutted a radiator once.

The autistic child is a lonely child, they say. Hampered at birth by strange compulsions, no matter how permissible the same behaviors would be in other children; defective in its fixation. It may, through struggle and sacrifice, brush up against some imitation of the joy normal children find in each other. But left to its own devices, it flounders in the swamp of its own mind, and is lost.

Go outside, they say, when the weight of the world presses down too heavily, and touch grass.

As a child, when I thought of grass, I mostly thought about the field that belonged to my primary school. I preferred the quiet little library corner inside the school, to be honest—windowless, dimly lit, a shelter from both the glare of the sun and the mocking laughter of classmates—and every once in a while had to be shooed away from it after lunch, not knowing at the time that teachers need breaks from students too.

Despite that, there were plenty of thoughts to be had about the field as well, if you knew where to look.

For a start: demographics. When the wooden fence traced its border between the school grounds from the surrounding village, each side it touched attracted a subtly different clientele. At the main gate, the soil was well trodden by the middle ranks of the school, the 7–8 year olds for whom the gate being unlocked every summer term was an event, but a familiar one: shoe prints, little footballs, an inexplicable crumpled pinafore, sprinklings of naked dandelion stems where the heads had been plucked and puffed away. Facing left from the entrance there and extending to the far side of the field, the older students would congregate in embryonic social packs to put as much distance as possible between themselves and the snot-nosed youngest kids still playing hopscotch and kicking stones around the playground proper, depositing little trails of plastic wrappers and squashed paper fortune tellers and lolly sticks when it was time to return to class. Along the right was a long strip of dry dirt where the grass came to a premature halt, blocked from the sun by a dense line of trees—and here, where the ground dipped to form a not quite child-sized hollow under the fence, was a post office for talking squirrels.

It turns out that demographics intersect with autism too. Since that time and place—my childhood in the late 1990s—much has been made of how underdiagnosed autistic girls, and autistic children socialized as girls, might be more inclined to self-soothe with escapist fantasy or popular media than the *Rain Man* facts and figures of their "male brain" peers suggest. A lot of it is blatantly gender essentialist; a nasty undercurrent of transphobia runs through it, churning sexist stereotypes into our already stereotyped "weirdness" in order to define us by our deviance, meeting the wide river of mainstream ableism at a muddy delta of eugenics. Those stereotypes were complications on my journey to a formal diagnosis years later, when I had to grapple with their underlying cruelty versus the liberation I felt when I saw some of my love of fantasy fiction in those escapism-obsessed caricatures—and yet not all of myself; when I came to realize that the simpler world the stereotypes painted didn't quite have space for all of me.

But down there in the dry dirt, small and prepubescent, comfortably removed from the cacophony of each class in each school day, I thought the world was simple enough. What's more, I had read and reread the copies of *Voyage of the Dawn Treader* and *The Silver Chair* I had at home enough times for my careless young thumbs to wear its illustrations of dragons, giants, and witches down to mere inky outlines of something fantastical. I thus understood that this post office was just one part of an expansive squirrel universe, but the squirrels were here nonetheless.

The story's simplicity did not mean it lacked history. A post office must come from somewhere, from its own time and place. I knew that the fence was the glass pane separating the staff from their customers, the tantalizing too-small hollow below was a slot for the dried-up autumn leaves they used as paper and the pebbles they used as money, the curiously flat-topped stone beside the hollow a weighing scale for bigger parcels such as a mitten with an L embroidered on the back, the dew-damp grass bordering the dirt the squirrels' welcome mat.

Some squirrels came by with important documents to sign, others to manage their bank accounts. When their business was done, they would dart back behind the fence outside the school grounds to homes unknown, to continue their happy family lives until the next lunch break when we were allowed back onto the field.

I knew, simultaneously, that I could never share these facts with another person. It's not that I didn't want to: see how charming the squirrels' tiny paws are, how fascinating their chittering little language, how bushy their tails! The biggest problem was that I was too tall to receive mail from the squirrels themselves, too inscrutable to belong with adults, and too weird to belong with other kids. How could I explain to them why I cared? All three groups would tell me I was foolish for caring.

Besides, like real post offices, it was rare for the squirrels to conduct their business without interference. Sometimes this came from inside, as it were: perhaps an ongoing subplot about the squirrels' various culture clashes with their coexisting local community of fairies, at other times a genre shift to a twisty-turny thriller about an invasion of snakes from outer space that were like the aliens in *Animorphs*, but cooler. Most of the time, however, the disruptions came from outside. When the bell rang for class and I was shuffled back indoors into the persona of the underachieving gifted child, the squirrels were gone. If the one person I considered a school friend collared me to talk about video games, or to pretend to be a goalpost in a game with his better friends, there would be no squirrel space in my head for at least the rest of the day. If I was too tense, perhaps from seeing some classmates walk by and remembering how they had laughed at me acting out some different story in some different corner of the playground, I would find the post office closed, forcing me to think of something else to do with my lunchtime.

Eventually we moved away, and I have no idea what that grassy school field has looked like since then. But the story carried on, through rain, and snow, and gloom of snakes.

* * *

Grass is a problematic plant, I learned as I grew up. Back in those days, when I would amble clumsily through the school field to reach the end of it and find some peace from the relentless noise, I never drew the connection between the grass and the hay fever sniffles I tended to suffer in the long months of the grass pollen season. Nor did I understand why it felt so difficult to walk across at times, unable to see the bumps and dips and unsavory leavings it was hiding from my careless feet. Grass is ubiquitous, and that makes it natural, because nature is socially defined. It doesn't matter that birds are more ancient than grass, which only embarked on its quest for world domination late into the time of dinosaurs, nor that the earth has spent the majority of its life adorned with no land plants at all, nor that the aesthetic desirability of carefully manicured lawns can turn huge swathes of land into essentially pesticide-drenched deserts devoid of native wildlife. Therefore, to have a problem with grass—to take issue with the pollen-choked sleepless summer nights, or the itchiness of mown grass blades on my skin, or the stains it left on the laundry—is to be unnatural, like the autistic child.

But grass is nice, if nothing is distracting you from appreciating it and you don't think too hard about what exactly might have pissed on it. The feel of the grass on the school field is an integral part of those childhood memories for me: a soft cushion to sit on while I watched the squirrels go about their work, a pleasantly cool texture between my fingers as I propped myself up in the sun, a splash of color to liven up the dry brown soil without overwhelming my senses like the classrooms indoors; a living thing to connect with, no matter how many eons apart we were.

Calm and simple as the world was in moments like those, I could not have remotely guessed at the sharper meaning that the phrase "touch grass" would pick up once I had become a terminally online adult. Today, it is a pithy admonishment, often directed at people considered too deep in their own post offices and their own squirrels: You care too much. You're too wound up. You're overreacting. Normalize yourself. Touch grass.

As a young person, clumsy with your emotions at best and outright unable to regulate them at worst, rejected by supposed friends for behavior you couldn't control, this can be a devastating blow. As an autistic adult, it is possible, if not always easy, to understand the assumptions baked into the suggestion and dismiss it when it does not fit. Everyone has a stress limit past which their emotions tumble out of control, and if autistic people experience that more often than allistic people, that indicates what a struggle it can be for us to find appropriately accommodating environments, rather than it being a personal fault. Everyone exists in systems within systems, in a time and a place.

There is at least one more assumption built into such a response, so broad as to map onto people's perceptions of autism as a whole: that things must be either problems or solutions, and so the world remains simple.

* * *

But my world didn't remain simple, because I grew up. Growing up meant adolescence, the period where the real world and its inherent noisiness grew too vast for me to keep up with, and where my body grew past the point where I could relate to it. In the shadow of adulthood, the kitschy fictional post office no longer had a place to open its doors; the stressors that used to disrupt the postal service from time to time multiplied and spread until they were my default state of being, as if my peers had all become tall enough to stare over my shoulder and point at me and mock me every minute of every day, while I was as tiny as ever inside an ungainly shell that I couldn't recognize as "me" no matter how hard I tried.

Even so, though many of my childhood memories of more embodied, physical things became hazy over time, the post office for squirrels remained in my head. So did the elaborate wartime tragedy of two particular Lego® pieces I had at home before losing them in the move, the eldritch-looking but friendly spirit who lived in the entryway of the local church, the garbled chorus of a song about a sentient island in a lake, and the cool snakes.

I liked writing fantasy stories in particular, I discovered. If the squirrels had no more stories for me, I would pen them myself. Swept up in the fixation on each fresh new idea, I could step out of my body for a time, plying it with cola and bland buttered toast just to keep it functional while I explored the times and places it was keeping me from.

The school field had become the hostile domain of PE teacher tyrants, so instead I hauled my cheap battered laptop between my darkened bedroom at home and an empty corner of the cafeteria, and spent my breaks tapping away at the keyboard.

Different themes took shape as my everyday struggles shifted and bent under the weight of the body dysphoria I began to experience in puberty. Several of the stories from this period involved teenagers unwittingly destined to turn into monsters of apocalyptic proportions over time, who managed to overcome their affliction through the power of friendship, and moved onto happier, almost anticlimactic lives. When they weren't straightforward fairytales, I would often try to build mystery plots in those settings, *Discworld* knockoffs that could be neatly resolved one day regardless of how messy the interim parts were. It's funny and enlightening to look back on those stories now through the lens of "write what you know," noticing all the patterns I was mired in as a teenager who thought myself uniquely unsuited to existence, too deep in those patterns to truly see them.

The one problem I did recognize at the time was that I couldn't step out of myself on demand. The ideas arrived or they didn't. Something as small as another kid imitating my clumsy shuffling walk or flat voice could sap the ideas away in an instant. True to the autistic stereotype, when there were no ideas to escape into, I had to stay in my shell, scant protection as it was from society's rejection of everything inside. Teenagers live and die by their social circles, but I didn't yet have the language to describe the kind of dysphoria I was experiencing, let alone friends I trusted enough to be an alternative outlet for it. There was only the shell, suffocating me in constant demands to perform femininity and neurotypicality, while still so thin and useless that everyone outside seemed to see right through it. Though on the outside I grew older, the shell tightened around the "me" inside until I could barely breathe. Only those fantasy stories were strong enough to punch air holes in it for a time, and so I continued to fear sharing them with other people, in case they punched back and left me defenseless.

After a while, even when the stories came to me, the shell was too tight for me to let them out. I had to go to university, had to keep my life on track, had to be presentable in order to survive. Besides, fantasy stories were childish and could not adequately address the complexities of the looming adult world in the way I thought math and technology could. I tried to ignore the shell, aiming what little focus I could muster at my studies and grades instead.

In retrospect, I should have known it wouldn't work. The notion of functioning "normally" enough to earn a reprieve from life someday was as much of a fantasy as the rest, and a more toxic one than most. Trying to mask as a functional allistic person only drained the energy I had channeled into my stories before, leaving them joyless and formless.

No post office is large enough to serve the whole world. By the time I crashed and burned out of my postgraduate studies, I had not written anything substantial outside of coursework in years.

* * *

I didn't seriously seek an autism diagnosis until I had exhausted my ability to mask, and even now it is a learning process. The term "autistic" itself is a mutable definition, a process arising from external mostly neurotypical factors; at its root it suggests isolation, a person defined by the quality of turning inward. It's most likely here to stay for lack of better alternatives, but nevertheless, that part of this particular social definition is odd to me—"neurodivergent" is ostensibly an umbrella term that includes autism, but that term only has meaning in contrast to the term "neurotypical," none in isolation.

Meanwhile, I exist inside a multitude of systems, and those include ecosystems. Introduce too many cane toads, and the delicate balance is thrown off; the native wildlife can no longer prosper. Pipe in too much sound, or too little motion, and similarly the complex web of my consciousness ends up in tangles large and small.

It was only natural that when I finally realized I needed to puzzle these systems out, it took some years of research and detective work before I knew where to start. I had not looked inward enough. The fantasies I loved so much had grown out of the experiences I had lived, the media aesthetics I had worked through, the struggles I faced. The post office had had a message to deliver to me all this time: I had never been a fool for caring about it. It was a creativity that could only flow if I, without fear or judgment, cared about myself.

* * *

I am older now, with its attendant freedoms and responsibilities. Stress still has a hold on me as an autistic adult; as long as noise and judgment and pollen allergies exist, it always will. I can't fully recapture that quiet sunny afternoon when I sat in the shade of the fence and observed the post office for squirrels. I don't think that I would want to, either—to throw away these hard-won scraps of understanding, and the people I finally found I belong to, for the sake of one moment in a life brimming with moments.

But I remember that afternoon whenever I reject the notion that respite is something to be left until the breaking point, or something to be sought only so I can work all the more efficiently afterwards. I remember it on the days when the adult obligations pile up like weights, when even survival feels like too much to ask of me, when any measure of peace feels as fictional as the squirrels, and all societal fictions feel as if they are for other people. I remember to afford myself room to breathe, to invite the fantasy stories unashamed for at least a moment every day. Fiction is a process, I must remind myself. That its end products appear simpler than the real world does not make it more simplistic, less useful. Fictions come from somewhere too, from times and places, from problems and desires and needs. Today, I know that fiction does not need to neatly solve my problems before it can help, or soothe, or nurture. Like my autism and my gender, it only needs to be.

I step outside, unbidden, and I touch grass. I situate myself in the sensation of swaying, in the comfortable clothes on my skin, in the breeze that murmurs a familiar song, in this time and this place. I listen, and the stories—like this one—go on.

The Joy of Sorting, Organizing, and Lining Things Up

Laura Kate Dale

One of the most difficult things about explaining autistic joy to non-autistic people, in my experience, has always been trying to work out how to separate the things I love from the clinical and medical language a doctor might use in a medical report, were they to observe those activities in a child.

There is perhaps no topic on which I have struggled with this question more than trying to explain why I love sorting, organizing, and lining things up.

Described in diagnostic criteria using stigmatizing labels like compulsion, which imply an inability to resist a damaging or meaningless activity or ritual, doctors will clinically assess that an autistic child organizes their possessions to gain a sense of control and normalcy in a chaotic world, and there is some truth to that assessment for sure, but to me that kind of description has always felt like it lacks the beauty and serenity that can be present in the act, one which can be chosen and desirable rather than simply a necessary mechanism of survival.

While I don't have clear memories of a lot of my childhood, I do have clear memories of organizing my toys at a young age. Sometimes it was a response to stress and unpredictability, but often it was an enjoyable act, valued for its own sake.

When you own a lot of something, it can be easy to forget exactly what that collection contains, and easy to fail to properly appreciate each component of a collection. Perhaps in part I feel this way because I also have aphantasia, a lack of visual imagination, and attention deficit hyperactivity disorder (ADHD), which impacts my object permanence. If something is out of sight, it's out of mind, and easily forgotten entirely in the moment.

Some of my earliest memories of lining up my toys in neat little rows were about remembering, appreciating, and understanding the objects I had around me. I could sort my Power Rangers Megazords by size, color, function, release date, or any other number of criteria. This was an act that required consideration and care, memory and feeling. Sometimes there would not be a clear numerical way to sort a category, such as which order to use if arranging objects by color. I could trust my instincts, then examine why I made the choices I did. It wasn't simply imposing order on chaos, but examining the unwritten rules I had somehow picked up and internalized, trying to put words to the ways my brain had decided chaos could be wrangled.

As I grew a little older, I moved from sorting toys to sorting trading cards. I would lay out huge numbers of *Yu-Gi-Oh!* cards on my bedroom floor, each neatly spaced, and take them all in at once, as a whole grand tableau.

Yu-Gi-Oh! as a game requires crafting a deck of cards from a very large pool of possible options, and in a world and a game with so many choices that things often felt overwhelming, there was something beautiful about being able to step back and see the entire picture, considering each choice in context. Each card picked up and selected was deliberate, requiring effort to navigate toward and add to my deck. Choices couldn't be made lightly without disrupting the neatly organized floor of cards, and so each choice carried weight and felt significant.

By lining things up precisely, the choice to disrupt that precision took effort. I had to be willing to take something out of this perfect pattern, and think about why I was doing it, and what value it would bring.

Once I was done, I would neatly sort the unchosen cards back into their box, ready to repeat the act again with each desired revision of the deck between sessions playing. It was an act of care and attention, one that felt like taking time for myself, that nobody else got to control but me.

As an adult, my outlet for sorting and organizing has very much become *Pokémon*, and my ever-growing collection of shiny color variant creatures. I am around 900 species deep into a quest to have one of every single shiny *Pokémon* that has ever existed, and that collection requires organization, maintenance, and manual curation.

Many of these *Pokémon* were caught in different games from each other. Many were caught by me, while many were traded from other players' collections. Some are in copies of the *Pokémon* games and in active use, while others share a large series of digital boxes they are stored in. There's no good way to automatically organize these creatures, and even if there was I would not make use of it. I enjoy the act of manually checking the order that *Pokémon* appear in the Pokédex, checking each of the locations I might have one of them in shiny, moving it into its proper place, marking it off on a spreadsheet, and progressing.

Any time I find an unexpected duplicate shiny *Pokémon*, and find I've not left a space for it in my collection, I manually shift many of my 900 creatures around to make a spot, enjoying the rhythmic act of shifting boxes and boxes of creatures one space to the right to leave a new gap. I enjoy the excuse to revisit each creature, seeing reminders of when and how I found it, be that a memory of an exciting capture catching me off guard, or a trade with someone willing to part with a rare creature to help my quest.

Lining things up, sorting them, and organizing them is a deliberate act of care to me. It's an act of observing something as it is, as part of a larger whole, and making sure it has a perfect place to be. It's about carving out a niche, so an object, or trading card, or digital creature is perfect, just where it is, and just how it is.

As someone who grew up feeling out of place, I feel like organizing and lining things up is an act of self-care. I didn't have a place I could fit neatly. But, when I sort things, I feel like every lined-up item has a spot where it perfectly belongs.

House Rules

Alastair Motylinski

A transgender author who spawned in a damp North Carolina basement in the mid-1990s.

When I was 16 I learned a very dangerous piece of information: the storage space in the outdoor carport, which was accessible via a flimsy pulldown ladder, contained a narrow opening to the interior attic. Anyone who wanted to break into our house could use it as an entry point, if they didn't feel inclined to put a brick through a window.

My mother told me of this connection in the same hushed tone she uses to point out protruding shirt tags on strangers in public. "Just in case anyone overhears," she whispered, though we were standing in our living room with the windows closed. There was an implicit warning in her tone: even though the attic passageway existed, I was not, under any circumstances, to attempt to use it. Naturally, I had never wanted to do anything more in my life.

I love being left unsupervised. It allows me to fuck things up with joyous impunity. If there is a social contract, its clauses may be freely ignored under circumstances of solitude. Rules may be forgotten, addendums overthrown, stipulations disregarded. Solitude is my preference over any other state of being, because it makes ample space for wondrous experimentation.

When I am not under observation, I do things which, were they observed, would generate weapons-grade amounts of secondhand embarrassment. Some of my activities are harmless: I sing loudly and off-key to Imagine Dragons on the interstate. I talk to myself. I slide across the linoleum in thick socks and go careening into laundry-closet doors. I visit the same trees in the neighborhood on every evening walk and greet them aloud by the names I gave them.

My other ventures are generally unwise and, at times, head-scratchingly devoid of sense. For instance, I love to go on walks during active thunderstorms. I am, against all evolutionary impulses, curious about hornets' nests. And I was desperate to break into my own house, if only to see if it was possible.

Thankfully, I did not have to wait long for an opportunity. My tendency to misplace vital objects—keys, wallet, glasses, shoes, phone—has been a point of consternation for my parents since I was old enough to leave the house. In this case I got home from school one afternoon in late August and realized I'd left my house key in the countertop salad bowl, buried under stretched-out hair ties and expired pizza coupons. I won't say I left it there on purpose, but my mother was not home, and I was alone, and I needed to get inside somehow. This was the moment I had longed for.

Breaking into a carport attic is easy, provided you don't mind being covered in spiders. The space within was murderously hot and stiflingly dark. I used my phone as a flashlight to verify it contained no mummified corpses or rabid animals, which at the moment were the only two things I was actually concerned about. The passage through to the attic was a narrow beam across a sea of fluffy pink insulation. About 20 feet away, beneath the eaves, I could just make out the suitcases we had taken on a trip to England the previous summer. Now they were mouse hotels.

Here is the thing about common sense: people tend to assume you have some. Apparently life comes with an invisible handbook, and it is embarrassing to admit to anyone that you never received your copy in the mail. There are certain things—such as swearing in public, eating during a phone call, and breaking into your own home through the attic—which a polite and civilized person simply doesn't do. Apparently there is a section on doing laundry in a timely manner and appendices on cooking rice. I don't know; I've never seen it.

Now here is the thing about insulation: it is begging to be stepped on. I thought it would feel like walking on a cloud. Like clouds, however, insulation is not solid.

Most people know this.

My leg plunged through the ceiling up to my hip. A rusty nail autographed my thigh. Chunks of plaster and a cataract of dust showered my stepfather's desktop PC with a thick layer of confectioner's sugar. Shifting my leg, I could peer straight through the hole and down into the music studio.

I managed to extricate myself and scramble back out through the carport, where my mother found me sitting half an hour later, looking both intensely contrite and like I was trying to conceal a grin. There was a part of me that had always wanted to put my foot through a ceiling, and the experience had been everything I hoped it would be.

"Why didn't you just call me?" my mom kept asking in a soft, heartbreaking voice. "There's a hole in the ceiling. Why didn't you just call?" To which I wanted to reply that I had been more than capable of putting the hole in the ceiling by myself, without anyone else's help. The truth, however, was that it had never once occurred to me to use my phone as anything other than a flashlight. I had resisted having a phone for years, because of the expectation that, once you owned a phone, you were going to use it to talk to people. I didn't need that kind of pressure in my life.

Even if I had thought of calling for help, I probably wouldn't have. I prefer to get up to my own nonsense. There is a wondrous joy that comes with solitude, and it is the freedom to be egregiously strange without worrying that you are committing some kind of social transgression.

Being one of those people who missed the handbook, I've had to learn the rules on my own. Whenever I am around other people, I make notes in my head. It amounts to a vague stream of distant observations that would not be out of place in an Attenborough nature documentary. Three healthy young males engage in a bonding exercise by etching depictions of their own genitalia onto their desks. Hilarity ensues.

When I was a kid, social engagement was an endless and frustrating game that was exhausting to play and seemed to have no natural solutions. Whatever I tried, I was still playing it wrong. My attempts at jokes dwindled into uncomfortable silence. The topics I chose for conversation were of no interest to anyone but me. I laughed too loudly and cried too easily. I heard from everyone that co-op was the superior way to go about life, but I still preferred the single-player mode.

As far as parents and peers were concerned, my preference for solitude was a problem which needed to be addressed. People tried to help me, of course. Girls made grudging room for me at the lunch table, invited me to their sleepovers, and came over to my house to play. One of them begged to go home early after she found me under the bushes behind the house, eating fallen leaves out of a salad bowl.

My mother, in particular, was bursting with suggestions on ways I could be less detestable. My intensity was unapproachable. I wore my makeup wrong. I dressed like a lesbian and walked like a boy. Some of this, at least, was prophetic—I transitioned to male not long after my 25th birthday. When I switched schools three times in sixth grade, my mom was overflowing with ideas: "A fresh start is a great opportunity to completely reinvent yourself! You can make a whole new you!" I could sort of appreciate her vision, but I do wish she hadn't been so enthusiastic about it. I had always been told that the most important thing to be was yourself, but now I was getting some contradictory messages. Clearly, something wasn't working out.

I did my best to abide by her advice, if for no other reason than because I thought it might make her happy. Turns out, I was a quick study. I learned how much eye contact to make with a stranger, the right way to arrange my face after receiving terrible news, and how to hold my hands inoffensively.

Each interaction with other people required immense emotional bandwidth as, moment to moment, I ran the calculations for the minutiae of tone, expression, and body language. There's a razor-thin margin for error. A social encounter felt like stuffing myself into a pillowcase. Tucking away flopping corners and unwieldy softness. Zip it up, zip it up, be neat and firm. I longed to ooze all over the place like a splodge of pancake batter. To laugh too loud and step on insulation and flail my arms and swear. To transgress, indulgently.

There was an unspoken house rule when I was growing up: no swearing. These days I think that fuck is the most beautiful word in the English language, but when I was young it was discouraged on a level somewhere between elbows on the table and curiosity about atheism. With my constant practice to suppress my natural social impulses, I had developed an intense sense of self-control. From the moment I learned (1) the existence of fuck and (2) its extraordinary power, I struck it forcefully from my vocabulary. I would go so far as to say I brainwashed myself. The mere thought of twisting my lips into the sound, of grazing my lower lip with my teeth in the beginnings of that most delicious F, struck me with a kind of Pavlovian nausea.

I was so proud of my overdeveloped sense of self-discipline that I bragged to my nanny. "I can't even think of swearing," I said. "It offends me." As if this made me a paragon of moral virtue—a good girl. I sat up straight. Elbows off the table. Mouth clean, pristine, unsullied.

Here was the truth, of course: I wanted to swear. I wanted it like cotton candy, chocolate cake, macaroni and cheese. I forbade it to myself: it was never an explicit conversation my parents needed to have with me. I had spent so long building my own set of rigid house rules that restricting my own language was second nature by now. I could play conversations the way some overachieving kids play the piano, stiffly correct and utterly passionless, but underneath I still felt a rhythm. It was different, and incorrect, and mine.

My parents had irregular work hours and were often unavailable to observe me, and I had no siblings, so I enjoyed the luxury of long periods of solitude. In the years since my childhood, my mother has apologized profusely for what she perceives as social neglect, but I doubt I ever would have found myself if I had not been given those long, quiet hours, when the noise of the world fell away and I could hear my own inner voice whispering to me, just loud enough to listen.

Who knows who I might have been if other people's words had filled me up, and left no space for solitude? Someone else, I imagine, though undoubtedly I would have kept my preference for weighted blankets.

So one day I was alone. I was on the front porch with a bowl of shrimp ramen and an orange soda, which are two of the worst flavors you can put in your mouth at the same time. The trees rustled in a warm summer breeze, and it seemed to me that they were murmuring, though I could never quite make out the words. There was nothing special about that day except that it was quiet, and my hearing was keener than usual.

"Hey," said the trees, or maybe it was my own subconscious, "do you know that in all your time on planet Earth, you have never once said 'fuck?'"

Again, the nausea, and its undercurrent: temptation. The siren song of untrod insulation. And because I was alone, I let my rules relax.

I whispered it, to start with: "Fuck."

Dear reader, there is nothing else in the world like saying fuck out loud for the first time. It's a high I will chase forevermore.

I giggled. I looked over my shoulder. I slurped my soup, and I said it again. "Fuck."

Sheer ecstasy. Through mouthfuls of noodles, I swore in every permutation of tone I could imagine, every declension and tense. Fucking and fucked and fucks and even some that I made up on the spot, fucky and fucko and fuckuckuckuck. I embellished my demented birdsong with other untasted words, too, like shit and piss and ass. I trod every forbidden inch of my vocabulary in a burst of delirious wanderlust.

Soon my soup was gone and I had to zip myself back up again and return to my eternal social calculus, but I had unearthed a priceless treasure: the true pleasure of my own company. It couldn't be taken away from me. It was not an avoidance of other people—there is an idea about solitude that it must be some kind of absence. For me, the right solitude is full and rich. I am a companion without rules or transgressions. When swearing lost its newness, I transitioned to saying other secret messages aloud, delivered from my lips directly to my ears:

Memorandum: The things no one else can see are still real.

Memorandum: You didn't do anything wrong. It's okay, it's okay, it's okay.

Memorandum: I love you no matter what you do.

Memorandum: He, him, his, Alastair.

Amazing how some problems go away the instant you stop trying to solve them.

When I had my top surgery earlier this year, a double mastectomy to masculinize my chest and rid me of a pair of extra considerations that had plagued me from the age of 14, I accidentally let myself out of the pillowcase. Some people will say anything under general anesthesia.

There is no room for curated personalities or real-time calculations. In vino veritas, as they say, and in anesthesia, candor.

My mom told me I regained rudimentary consciousness and launched straight into an improvised comedy routine. It must have been halfway coherent, because at least one nurse had to leave the room and the surgeon, my mom told me, was fighting back a grin as he gave her my post-operative care instructions. I don't remember any of that. When I came to, I had exactly one thought pinging around in my brain: I was going to send a picture of myself to everyone I knew, with the caption: I lived, motherfucker. Don't ask me why—I think it was a knee-jerk jubilation—but it turns out this is not a good text to send to your stepfather.

When I did pull myself together an hour or two later, it was with the dawning sense that I had done something catastrophically embarrassing. My mother revealed that my comedy routine had been explicit: "Every other word out of your mouth was the F word," she told me in soft horror. "I've never heard you talk like that."

Even my stepdad primarily expressed confusion: "It just really surprises me."

I soon gave up trying to argue the point. It's difficult enough, under the best of circumstances, to explain your unfiltered self to someone who all along thought you were someone else. It is impossible to do it lying in bed like a cicada husk, high on oxycodone and dribbling out the corner of your mouth.

It was just that, for a little while, I had spoken to everyone else the way I speak to myself. It felt like confirmation that my natural dialect required translation, which I provide pro bono, every conversation, transposing painstakingly in real time like a beleaguered musician moving notes from treble to bass.

"That's just how I talk," I wanted to say. "That's just how I talk, for real." But that isn't true—I do not go around habitually swearing at strangers. It's just how I would talk if I were by myself all the time, which, let's be frank, sometimes I wish I could be.

Not very long ago, I locked myself out of the house again. I had gone for an evening walk to a little-known spot in my neighborhood, an abandoned lot between houses where a shallow creek bent its elbow around a stand of young white oaks. I go there a lot to be alone with them. I crouch in the leaf litter and watch tiny fish dart around a chunk of collapsed pavement for a while, and then I touch every tree—just to remind them we both live on earth—and then I stroll along home. On this particular evening I was reaching for the doorknob when I remembered my keys were still hanging on the hook inside.

The situation was dire. Night had already fallen, and the carport light was off. My mom and stepdad would not be home for hours yet, and what's more, I had left my phone behind. I was utterly alone.

I milled around in the yard for a few minutes. Then I went and laid down on the sloping driveway. I settled onto the cool, gravelly pavement and stared up, up, up at the gaps between the trees.

Softly and to myself, I whispered, "Fuck."

Happy Stimming

Laura Kate Dale

Of all the joys I find, day to day, in my life as an autistic adult, perhaps none were as hard fought for, or took as much mental unpacking, as letting myself flap my hands with joy, without shame or guilt.

As a young child, one of the first manifestations of my being autistic that my parents took notice of, even if they didn't realize it was a sign of autism, was my constant and hard-to-shake need to stim.

Stimming, or self-stimulatory behavior, is often talked about in diagnostic criteria surrounding autism in relationship to struggling and suffering. As autistic people, many of us struggle with unpredictability, be that in the form of changes to routine, unexpected and unpredictable sensory input, or overlapping sources of social demand. In those scenarios, actions that introduce predictable sensory input, such as hand flapping, spinning, or in intense cases head hitting can cut through the static, and introduce something predictable and stable to center on.

When I was growing up, my mother kept a journal, chronicling things she thought were notable during my formative years. While she may not have known it at the time, part of what she chronicled was my history of childhood stimming, and insights into how stimming was viewed in my household as I grew.

From an incredibly young age, I needed to stim. As an infant, it took the form of needing my hand rhythmically squeezed so I would stop crying and go to sleep. A few years later, it became rhythmically rocking myself. As I got closer to school age, my stims became more noticeable and pronounced, and my mother made attempts to curb the behaviors, so I would not be perceived as abnormal by my peers.

The problem is, starting school meant a huge increase in sensory input to deal with, and a whole lot more unpredictability introduced into my routine. As soon as my mother got me to stop hopping every third step, I started making beeping noises. As soon as that stopped, I started twirling my wrists repeatedly. Every time a stim was discouraged, a new one took its place to meet the needs I had for predictability in difficult settings.

The overarching message I got growing up was that stimming was to be discouraged, no matter the form it took. It obviously didn't stop me stimming, but it did force me to make my stims more subtle, and hide them in plain sight. Elastic bands worn around fingers and rotated, pens assembled and disassembled, tapping my legs, and rubbing my thumb with my index finger became the tools of choice, deployed when absolutely necessary.

Because of this minimizing of my own stimming, I never really gave myself room to stim as a joyous activity until my 20s, when I started to unpack the parts of myself that had been buried to survive as a child.

When people ask me to explain happy stimming, who are not themselves autistic, I tend to tell them that they're probably already familiar with the concept, under a different name. Jumping for joy.

When a non-autistic person uses the phrase "jumping for joy," while it might be a metaphor of sorts, it is in some cases very literal. When a person is so overloaded with excitement, happiness, and elation, they sometimes find the need to physically let it out by jumping up and down, running up to a friend to hug them, or even just vibrating a little in place. While it's not one to one, the experience of happy stimming is remarkably similar.

I've always had trouble regulating my emotions, and positive emotions are honestly no different. Sometimes, when I am overcome with happiness, it feels like it's going to consume me the same way sensory overload might, as I get lost in the happiness overloading me. It needs an outlet, and one it can predict and rely upon.

While it took a long time for me to feel safe to indulge that sensation—guilt and shame took a long time to unpack—now I let my hands flap up and down, let myself spin around in circles, bounce my legs up and down, or rock side to side when I am at my happiest. It acts almost like a feedback loop, reinforcing the positivity I feel, while keeping it controllable. I let my joy out physically, and the freedom I feel is freeing, adding to the joy I feel in the moment.

Happy stimming is, for me, a twofold act. It's about not trying to suppress an expression of joy, but it's also about sharing that joy with others. When I am so happy I could burst, I love that the people closest to me can see that. I love that I don't need to feel ashamed at my happiest, and that my joy no longer needs to go through a filter before it's ready to see the light of day.

Everything but the Kitchen Sink

Elsa Monteith

The kitchen

My evenings of autistic joy are often hosted in my dimly lit kitchen, a narrow room filled with soft golden shadows, accompanied by the rumble of the kettle reaching a mild and pleasing crescendo. I find great joy in cooking, the fragrant cardamom pods crushed by a heavy pestle and mortar for an elaborate meal, balanced by the rhythmic stir of soup from a tin for the evenings of freezer bread and no butter. These are gentle and regular joys I share with myself and my patient housemate, a quiet ode to my autistic joy and the pleasure I take in harmless habits and neurodivergent rituals.

Being autistic brings with it many sensory challenges. Food presents a vast disparity of texture, taste, and touch, serving up a plate piled high with potential distress for neurodivergent people who struggle with difference. Eating when autistic can look like a distinct resistance towards the unknown dish sat in front of you, or an ardent desire for the chosen seat at the dinner table that's already occupied. It could be an intolerance for the clatter of plates being noisily stacked up ready for the sink, or the unbearable stench of a no-thank-you food that remains in the upper echelons of your nasal cavity all evening.

It's hard, it's overwhelming, and it often leads to discomfort, distress, and, more often than not, meltdown.

I've been reckoning with the intricacies of food for my full quarter of a century of living, an experience that's at once a wholly universal and deeply personal activity. I've been feasting on this frustration for as long as I can remember, interrogating how my autistic identity grapples with the grit and grub we consume more than three times a day, and how to clean up afterwards.

All too often, however, we focus on sensory overwhelm, and not what can happen when we harness the circumstances that cultivate peace and nourish joy. To me, in all its complexity, cooking is a compendium of autistic joy, rooted in sensory difference and a love for a practice that repeats itself by rote.

I hope to linger a little longer at the open door of the fridge, sifting through the jars of mustard I will never eat, and some unidentifiable citrus fruit that I have no memory of buying. I want to experiment with what food and cooking can mean for autistic people, whilst acknowledging the depth of difference we experience, and the privilege I hold. This chapter makes space on the counter for neurodivergent people to explore their connection with the kitchen, to invent new ways to identify with cooking, and to see what's still on their plate.

The recipe book

The recipe books I thumb through are well loved and well used. I rotate between perhaps three core texts, as well as dipping in and out of newspaper cuttings and the scribbled old-hand recipes penned by my mum. To me, recipes can become quite fantastical, conjuring up vast cauldrons of broth, or magic porridge pots to satiate an expansive autistic imagination. Little does she know, but Rukmini Iyer has had a seat at my table for the past six years, her *Green Roasting Tin* cookbook acting as a vegetarian gospel underpinning a good 60 percent of my meals. Unbeknownst to him, Nigel Slater's lyrical seasonal recipes guide my autumn, while Ruby Tandoh's honest and frank food writing brings the best out of my cupboards, tins, and long-forgotten jars all year round.

Sometimes the best meals require no recipe. My not quite so halcyon days of being skint at university often called for a tin of knock-off Heinz cream of tomato soup, delivering a glistening titian bowl of steaming goodness that would first burn my tongue, and then help to calm my overwhelmed head thick with exhaustion. Having just one instruction, "heat," gave me clarity in years of confusion, where "chop," "slice," or "simmer until translucent" would have sent me over the edge. Soup is a cheap meal, and crucially, reliable. Every tin looks, feels, and sounds the same, with every humble can of beans, peas, or other nondescript pulse delivering exactly what's promised (on the tin). As I see it, there's a quiet nod to neurodivergent needs here, a serving of sameness, housed in corrugated silver, and wearing a label with precise numbers, digits, and figures.

I was lucky to grow up in a home with a selection of tins to choose from, stacked up high on the shelf above the fridge. I would drag up a chair and peruse my options, admiring the coveted Del Monte tinned peach slices and the curiously green Green Giant sweet corn. There's a charm and wit in the design of tin can labels, with one particularly famous tin of Campbell's tomato soup becoming the face of contemporary UK art in the 1960s. At the helm of this movement is repetition, a deliciously autistic way of thinking, acting, and being.

Recipes are a fascinating way of creating something repeatable, flavorsome. A good recipe leaves room for experimentation and invention, whilst retaining the integrity of an achievable and replicable dish. The autistic need for reliability in cooking and eating can evolve into something of a science; we can observe the rolling boil of salted water meeting 80 grams of dried pasta, whilst a dash of salt combines seamlessly with a lick of oil and two crushed cloves of garlic in a heavy lidded pan. We can notice the way the juices coalesce, leaking from one into the other and back again. Or—when we haven't got the time, resources, or energy—we can make toast.

The kettle

For me, being autistic is to be acutely aware of my surroundings, sensitive to minute changes, and, crucially, the availability of the correct teaspoons for tea-brewing purposes. Having a harmless ritual or routine is something to be celebrated. I am an expert in how I take my tea; I know how much milk is too much, what shade of foggy brown my mug must adhere to, and the exact temperature that justifies the first sacred sip. I know that my chamomile tea must only be sipped after 9 p.m., and that out of the many beloved mugs that grace the shelf, there's a specific time and place for a select few of them. It's a skill to know yourself and your preferences, to know how to concoct a mug of tea to warm you or settle yourself at times of stress. For each and every one of us, neurodivergent or not, holding something between our hands can be grounding, enlightening the senses of touch, taste, and smell.

As is the case for much of the population, I find myself padding over to the kettle many times a day. The well-rehearsed dance of lid open, tap faucet on, click back, and wait is a comfort, and a signifier that I'm in need of some caffeine, or company. There are myriad ways to make a cup of tea: milk first, steeped in a teapot, just below boiling, or a simple builder's brew. These requirements are highly attuned and different for each and every tea drinker, sipper, or slurper. It brings joy; a simple way of gesturing comfort.

I've always been curious about good manners. Why is offering someone a cup of tea considered polite? The whys and wherefores of acceptable guest-based conduct is a fascinating observation in human behavior. For some, the "Would you like a cup of tea?" reflex comes naturally, an intuitive greeting, but for many autistic people the meanings behind these customs aren't as clear.

Tea time in fiction has always been a good point of reference for me—Paddington Bear's "elevenses" with Mr. Gruber deliver a quiet nostalgia, as do the dreamlike tales by Beatrix Potter painting simple comforts of "bread and milk and blackberries for supper" for Peter Rabbit and his sisters. I've always been drawn to the word "Fika" for these moments, a Swedish term that roughly translates to "making time for friends and colleagues to share a hot drink and have a little something to eat."[1] It's customary, and it's cozy, and lends itself well to an autistic sensibility.

The table

The quaint unwritten rules of hosting can easily be interpreted as an autistic fever dream—the case-by-case customs of a household that don't always translate to your neighbor's front room or colleague's doorstep can cause sensory havoc. Bright lights have always presented issues for me and a lot of the autistic community, with acute sensitivity to sensory experiences that lean into extremes. What I thought of as a universal "dim light policy" has not got the widespread support

1 Elizabeth Hotson (2016) Is this the sweet secret to Swedish success? BBC Worklife. Accessed March 24, 2022 at www.bbc.com/worklife/article/20160112-in-sweden-you-have-to-stop-work-to-chat

I had initially expected, with many homes and public spaces opting for the brightest, whitest, easiest, and quite often cheapest lighting option. Entering into a new space or "dinner party forecourt" brings with it a new and nerve-wracking series of unknowns; will they want me to take my shoes off? What does it mean to "mingle"? How can I leave early? I never thought I'd have the understanding, or autonomy, to create a space that was gentle, soft, and welcoming, either to the needs and wants of my own identity, or to those I ask to join me.

In my case, the joy of inviting friends new and old into my home to share a table and a meal with me has shaped a neurodivergent infatuation with homely habits and domestic traditions. Inviting someone into my narrow, cozy kitchen marks a crossing of thresholds—I pull up extra folding chairs to a table barely fit for two, weighed down by elaborate crowdsourced dishes and the cheapest screw top Pinot Grigio which tastes remarkably like vinegar. Hosting is like "playing house" for me, a curious intersection of learnt manners meeting pretense. Amongst friends, etiquette dissipates. Formalities resolve into a mutual understanding that eye contact is not necessary, and an early night is appreciated.

In many ways, I see hosting as a short-lived and abbreviated exercise in sensory accessibility. When bringing people round the table to share food, I ask in advance for their dietary requirements and personal preferences, negotiating a menu that appeals to a variety of palates and inclinations. I curate a playlist that bends to their taste, and design a space that balances low, glowing, golden light with carefree conversation and a pack of cards. As hosts of intimate DIY dinners, it is our responsibility to accommodate, facilitating the breaking of bread and joining of like-minded friends. We are sensitive to the desires of our guests, and fine-tune the room to meet them. We find ourselves saying things like "Are you comfortable?" or "Can I get you anything?" and begin to learn that perhaps we should be asking ourselves the same questions.

The washing up

I haven't always loved washing up. My first job at 15 was at a cafe where I spent much of my time dunking faux vintage cups and saucers into warm soapy water for £4.50 an hour. After some time I became an expert in washing logistics, enlisting my colleagues to dry up and replace crockery onto their shelves while I furiously scrubbed, cleaned, and rinsed. On busy days I would run the taps and devise the drying rack system that blew any competition out the water. A year later and I had found comfort in the quiet focus I had developed with my back to the world. The sink became my domain.

Washing up is like the end credits of a film. As they roll down the screen, we rinse off suds and place utensils upside down to drain. As taps pour steamy running water, we signal the end of a meal, returning plates, glasses, and a resplendent range of (often unused) cutlery to their respective homes. Saying that, sink habits vary greatly from household to household—dirty dishes can remain on counter tops for many days, or be held to a stringent family regime of washing up any remnants the second the last morsel has been eaten.

I, like many, end my meal with the washing up. I enact a rinse-before-wash practice, and fill the bowl with water just hot enough to make my fingertips tingle. For me, it's a sensory joy, a fragrant bath for my hands repeatedly circling dishes with a soft sponge below the water line. I love the consistency of it all, a habitual repetition. The muffled jingle of forgotten cutlery accompanied by the quiet thud of a chopping board hitting the plug brings with it a bizarre type of submerged pleasure. I have agency over the temperature and control of the taps—I can decide on what meets my sensory needs and enjoy the bubbles that belch from the bottles that sink to the bottom of the bowl.

There are days when I would do anything to avoid the stacked-up plates and oily roasting tin that has seen better days. It's a chore and a bore, and without company or a podcast it can be mind-numbingly dull. It's times like these that call for an alternative perspective to the cryptic (and perhaps optimistic) mystique of washing up. You heard it from me first; radical self-acceptance is the new joie de vivre—it's okay to do it in the morning.

The takeaway

I am a culinary romantic. I see the act of washing up as akin to a fairytale soap opera, and can, with ease, write a lyrical ode to the art of feeding friends. Cooking is a love story, one that leans into the senses, and take value from comfort. It's a practice built on care, and follows a domestic gesture towards sharing and generosity, whatever your means.

More often than not, the takeaway is the remedy. The arrival of tepid plastic containers slick with grease accompanied by the knowledge that there's no washing up is a moment of untold pleasure. It's a delicious and deserved indulgence, and a stoic reminder that cooking can look like a Deliveroo transaction if you really want it to.

Cooking is complex, and can be unpredictable—the smolder of charred burnt toast isn't always in our control, and the egg timer won't always chime when it's most convenient. We won't always be able to afford the ingredients we desire, and many of us will be choosing between heating or eating when winter knocks on our doors. Sharing meals and moments creates joy for me, and when we don't have kitchen tables, we can congregate in other ways, splitting a Kit

Kat at the bus stop and taking turns to swig from a polystyrene cup filled to the brim with cheap sweet tea.

I find that autistic comfort is often about warmth and containment. There's something about being "held," or of "holding"; be it space, time, or a mug of tea, we are often seeking out an enduring and dependable calm. I surround myself with the food writing, recipe books and fiction that make me feel safe, and shape a kitchen space that welcomes friends and nourishes joy.

As we patiently observe the ways we cook, care, and share space, the kitchen follows form. The gentle, honest, and all-encompassing second home I find myself spending time in, honoring food with fondness, three times a day.

Infodumping

Laura Kate Dale

Growing up, I was taught that there are very strict and firm rules about how conversations are meant to be paced and structured.

Each person takes their turn, being careful not to monopolize the conversation. Don't change the topic of conversation without checking that is okay. Make sure you are making eye contact while you are listening, so they can see you are paying attention. Definitely keep an eye on the other person, and stop talking if they do not seem enthusiastically interested in the topic at hand.

It was that last rule that often tripped me up. I find it very hard at the best of times to know what other people are thinking, and even more than usual when I am excited about something I know lots about, and find super interesting.

As an autistic person whose special interests were often either considered childish, such as being obsessed with *Pokémon* still in my teen years, or niche and nerdy, such as being obsessed with the societal and social function of trains and other public transport, I often found that the things I was bursting to tell the world about, and the things people wanted to know about, didn't always line up.

This always confused me as a child, primarily because of the way I engaged with information, and other people's enthusiasm. I might not have a particular interest personally in 1980s pop bands, or the TV show *The Sopranos*, but if right now, you sat me down with an expert on either topic and prompted them to talk about why they love their respective topic, I would honestly have a great time. Enthusiasm is infectious, and to me there are few joys greater than watching someone who is genuinely enthusiastic about a topic explain why they love it.

I don't need to enjoy the subject myself; a person with sincere love for a topic will usually show you exactly what there is to love in it, if you give them a chance.

But, back to the past, my infodumping was usually met with at best disinterest, and at worst outright annoyance. People either were not interested in hearing about what I had to share, or were actively annoyed I had broken an unspoken rule by not realizing my conversation partner was disinterested and cutting myself off prematurely in response.

But, as I have grown older, and found increasing numbers of autistic friends, family, and partners to spend my life with, I have found that there are people who, like me, enjoy infodumping, regardless of the subject involved.

When my wife, Jane, and I first moved in together several years ago, we had both experienced a history of being shot down when we tried to enthusiastically share our interests with others. As a result, the first few months we were living together involved a lot of times where one of us would start enthusiastically explaining something, only to cut ourselves short, apologizing for taking up too much space in the discussion.

The thing is, each time the listener insisted it was okay to keep talking, and that they were genuinely enjoying listening, it got a little easier.

Each time, little by little, we as speakers felt safe to speak a little longer.

I may not know obsessive amounts about Transformers, and my wife may not know obsessive amounts about *Pokémon*. I may not know a lot about twisty puzzles, and she may not know a lot about *Yu-Gi-Oh!* cards. That doesn't matter at the end of the day, because when one of us starts enthusiastically sharing facts that we find exciting, the other locks in intently, ready to learn, because anything interesting enough to elicit that kind of enthusiastic energy is worth listening to, and supporting, and encouraging.

Where once I would have been ashamed to infodump, now I do so with joy, and confidence, unapologetically. To prove my point, I hope you will indulge me as I share a bunch of facts about a topic that my brain has a *lot* of information stored up about.

Yu-Gi-Oh! as a trading card game is somewhat unique in that it doesn't contain a "mana" system. Most trading card games have a form of energy, such as Lands in *Magic: The Gathering* or Energy cards in *Pokémon*, which are typically limited to the player only getting to use one per turn, controlling the pace that the game plays.

Yu-Gi-Oh!, in its early years, had an alternative to a mana system designed to control its pacing, summoning conditions. Players could only summon one monster per turn, limiting the pace at which the game could move, and setting a standard for how past players could advance their game state. There were occasional exceptions to this once per turn rule, called special summons, but these were the exception rather than the rule.

Over the years, however, *Yu-Gi-Oh!* has become a *much* faster game, with matches at competitions now taking often as little as two or three turns, because the game introduced more and more special summonable monsters, meaning that the one normal summon per turn rule became less and less of a restriction to the pace of the game. As a result, if you can find ways to draw cards, players can often have incredibly lengthy turns full of huge combos, as early as the first turn of the game.

This is part of why *Yu-Gi-Oh!* has, more than perhaps any other trading card game, accelerated in game pace over the past 20 years. The game's core mechanic for controlling game pace essentially no longer exists meaningfully.

See, even if you didn't know about any of that before, I hope it was a little parcel of interesting information. I find that fascinating, and I hope that translates into interest when reading too.

Infodumping is a joy for the speaker, and if you take the time to listen, it can be joy for the listener, witnessing passion at its purest.

Better than Super Smash Bros: School

Hanna Holland

My first memory of school is running out of my classroom, fear-stricken and alone. The teacher hadn't done anything as other students called me names, poked me with pins, and put peanut butter and jelly sandwiches on my chair. The stickiness had become a custom, and the shame a routine, but I had finally had enough.

I was found shortly after, my back and butt covered in purple stains, and reprimanded for crying. I lost recess privileges. I rode the bus home hoping I wouldn't stick to the seat. The whole time I wondered why my teacher, who was meant to protect me, had instead further hurt me.

My first memory ends like this: cheeks wet with tears and hands curled into fists, eyes scanning the lines of a history book about the Roman Empire, and the resounding decision that I would never go back to school after I finished compulsory education.

Many years later, there I was, the fall semester of my senior year of college, sitting in one of my professors' offices. My thesis was complete, my degree nearly finished, and I hadn't considered a career outside of pursuing graduate education in the classics. But the time had come, and I couldn't afford it.

I hadn't, until that point, really thought of a career beyond classics. Sure, I had enjoyed working with children in summer camp settings, having been a senior counselor and assistant. I'd even run my own summer camp with the assistance of a reading specialist, a reading development camp targeting under-privileged and low-income students with disabilities. Despite this, due to my trauma, I never considered childcare or child education as an option.

My professor walked into the room two minutes after me with an Arizona tea juice box and a cookie. She knew about my history, and knew about my love of children and working with kids with disabilities. She also knew I hadn't thought at all to work with kids as a career. Which is why, when she handed me the tea and half the cookie, the words she said changed my life.

"Have you ever thought of teaching?"

Despite my school-based trauma, from that moment in her office forward, I couldn't stop thinking about it. About teaching, about trauma, and about the other students who could be having experiences like I did. After a couple of months of thought on the subject, in January 2020, I decided that I could be the teacher for others that I'd needed.

I researched different post-baccalaureate teacher programs and found that the University of Pennsylvania had one. They placed you in a high-need, minority populated urban school, with very heavy support, after an intense spring and summer of courses, and a summer teaching assistantship within your content area. While in this school placement, you were expected to take night classes to complete your certification requirements at an accelerated rate. After I registered, and completed the intensive courses and teaching assistantship to pursue a certification in Special Education, I had an offer letter for a special education job teaching ninth-grade modified English to teenagers in an inner-city school in Kensington, Philadelphia.

And I was scared shitless.

I didn't want to impart the same trauma onto my students that had been imparted to me, and I had no clue how not to do that. All I wanted was to be the teacher they could be themselves with; to be the teacher who they would come to if they ever needed anything.

During my intensive study before I began, I realized that the subject matter of my certification was very close to home. All my studying during the intensive courses on disabilities, all the symptoms, all the signs—they added up to one thing: I had all the glaring symptoms of autism, and I'd majored in what was very clearly my special interest. Partially scared, partially relieved, I discussed it with my therapist, who referred me to a psychologist.

When I entered the classroom in September 2020, it was with a diagnosis newly in hand and fire in my blood. I was determined that none of my students would ever feel the way I did. I was determined that, if I could make one student feel safe and love learning again, I would be happy.

This, as all things, was easier said than done.

My first year of teaching was virtual. I lived in my apartment, and taught in my apartment, and cleaned in my apartment, and I never left my apartment. In some ways, this made it easy; I didn't have to worry about the same relationship-building I would have in a normal year. Yes, I talked to them, and supplied them with a safe space, and did my best to create an environment where my students felt capable and happy, but it was much easier to do this without being expected to make eye contact and have to manage a physical classroom with so many different personalities.

However, I really felt like I wasn't doing the thing I had set out to do. I couldn't give my students a physical safe place, couldn't give them a chance to know that I had their backs. I wanted to give them what I'd known so many other teachers had failed to give them, simply by virtue of having a disability in a public school: the feeling of safety in the classroom.

The next year was in-person. It was hard.

The first month, I wanted to quit every day. Because my students had been out of the classroom for 18 months, many of them with behavioral concerns related to trauma had lost a lot of progress in their academic and behavioral goals. The lack of in-person education had caused all of my students severe setbacks when they had already had low educational score levels prior to the pandemic due to a combination of their cognitive disabilities and systemic issues within the school system. Many of my students with autism appeared to be genuinely afraid of the classroom which, although likely not new, had certainly been exacerbated by the lack of classroom exposure. I had a lot of work to do.

There is a saying in teaching: "Don't smile until November."

What this means is that if you show any sort of understanding or kindness before November, the students will take advantage of you.

Other teachers laughed or scoffed at the way I interacted with my students from the start. I opened up my classroom for discussion of boundaries and respect and allowed my students to work in ways best for them, even when this didn't mean they would be seated and quiet like many other classrooms expected. My coworkers thought policies like this meant the students would walk all over me and have poor behaviors. In my opinion, this is an incredibly harmful, reductionist, and lazy thing to say. They're teenagers. Of course they're going to push boundaries. They're going to say mean things. They're going to try things out. That doesn't mean they don't deserve just as much care and respect as everyone else.

As the year went on, my students began talking about their interests to me, and began to open up more. The students who still pressed boundaries at least felt comfortable speaking in my class, when they started the year as quiet as ghosts. I noticed that students who had previously been terrified to complete work for fear of failure began to turn things in because they knew I'd always help them and give them chances to fix mistakes.

Right before winter break, a student approached me during my prep period and asked to talk. He was quiet, and sat in the back of the classroom. He had few friends, and he often played video games in class when he wasn't supposed to. This student has difficulty controlling his emotions, the good and the bad.

This student is the reason I'm teaching.

He asked me if I could play *Super Smash Bros*, a cartoonish fighting game, with him during lunch. I, of course, was more than happy to indulge in one of my favorite video games, and as we played, he talked. He talked more than I'd heard him talk the whole year. He told me about his hopes and dreams, and why he was afraid in school, and about his life outside of school. He told me about his grandparents, who raised him. He told me about the bullying he faced. He told me about growing up in an area stricken by an opioid epidemic and poverty.

Right before the bell rang, he told me that he liked my class best out of any class he'd had, and he turned in his very first assignment for the year. It was one from the first day of school. His handwriting was sloppy, and his spelling was poor. I looked at one answer in particular and had to hold in my tears until he left.

There, the question sat: Who is a favorite teacher you've had? Why were they your favorite? What sorts of activities did you do in their class?

There, the answer sat: Ms. Holand. She lisens to me. I lik wen she reeds to us.

It was then, fighting off tears, that I got the idea.

Yes, I listened to them, and yes, they knew I cared about them. They'd shown so much growth emotionally and academically. I was full of happiness, making excited noises in the back of my throat walking into school every day. I knew, though, that they deserved to have their voices heard by more than just me. I could already feel my hands flapping in excitement beneath my desk. For once, I didn't stop them.

I approached my students the next day with the idea of doing something that incorporated all the things they were interested in. Transit systems, painting, bumble bees, dinosaurs, and more. I asked them if they might want to paint a huge mural with me, allowing them to show everyone why they loved the things they loved. At first, they were understandably hesitant. Many had the preconceived notions that doing something like this would make them soft in the eyes of their peers. Many were ashamed of their interests, had been made to feel that they weren't important. But, over time, they grew warm to the idea. After some community meetings, some planning, and some very tense conversations with a few different building owners, we had picked out a spot. We fundraised for the materials, asked for volunteers, and eventually, finally, the day had arrived. There was a grassy area right next to this building, and a large swath of area for us to cover. The wall had already been covered with a bottom coat of paint from our adult volunteers, who'd done the groundwork for us.

The first student to take up a paint brush was, predictably, my student who couldn't be found without some sort of art supplies.

"I'm going to paint a paint brush. It's going to be ironic," she said to me, monotone, and I laughed. As soon as she got to work, I felt another student tap my shoulder. The one who had come to me during lunch.

"Can you help me paint Donkey Kong?" he asked quietly. His voice cracked a bit with nerves. His hands appeared to be shaking around the small brush he'd picked up. My voice cracked, too, when I responded.

"Of course. Could you help me paint Kirby?" I asked. He smiled at me, and the two of us began.

By the end of the day, my students had all contributed something. Our resident artist helped us make it cohesive, as did our other volunteers. We left feeling happy and excited, and for the first time ever, all of my students were talking excitedly with each other, not me, about the interests they'd only just been shy about. They were already asking me when our next painting session would be, and I was more than happy to tell them we could do this every Friday as far as I was concerned. I felt the grin on my face for a full five hours after that, thinking about them interacting with each other. There hadn't been a single moment of unkind words the entire time.

As the weeks went by and we got closer and closer to the finish line, I saw a change in so many of my students. Less fear in the classroom, and more confidence. I had to remind more and more students to raise their hands before shouting the answer. I had to tell many to keep their talking to a minimum, had to set up a classroom quiet board to incentivize quiet during instruction time. I was the happiest I'd ever been in my classes. During the day, I no longer hid my stims from my students. I talked openly about my autism, and excitedly discussed my special interest, classics, with them.

I also noticed a change in other classes. Students were making top grades in their classes despite all they had going against them. Teachers were telling me how much of a change they'd gone through, that their participation was at an all-time high.

Meanwhile, I kept teaching. Kept bridging the gap between the instruction they should have received, versus the instruction they truly got. We covered four years' worth of English topics during this time, from basic grammar to complex figurative language topics.

Finally, after about two months of painting, we had finished. The wall was covered in the things my students love. Some of the paintings were crude, with their edges fuzzy and their paint splattered. My student who loved art had managed to make it all look cohesive and intentional, and I caught her encouraging those with little art skill too many times to count.

After it was finished, we took a picnic there, in the tiny patch of grass next to the wall. As I looked at my students, talking and laughing and playing games, I felt my eyes tear up with the most unbridled joy I'd ever felt. I tried to wipe them away, but my students weren't having any of it. The boy who had barely spoken and barely turned in any assignments, patted my shoulder and told me that it was okay to cry. That I could trust him, that he wanted to return the favor.

My heart felt light and heavy at the same time, and I felt my fingers moving in a stim before realizing what I was doing.

The happiness you feel when you're around people you love, whose love you have earned with care, is indescribable. I truly love my students, in a way that is so complicated and inexplicable. We have very few ties aside from the relationships we developed that year, but somehow I feel more tied to them than people I've known my whole life.

The year ended how it began: with a quiet room dotted in spots of loudness. With games and nervous excitement. The quiet, however, was because we were all sad the year was ending. The loudness was no longer interruptions, but heated and excited discussions. The games were played with the competitive nature of a family, knowing they can be angry and upset and still be confident they're cared for. The nervousness wasn't due to newness, but anticipation and fear of what comes next. I know, in my heart of hearts, that I will always love them, and that they know they can always come to me.

The boy who speaks a lot and yet not at all walks through my door the next year, on the first day of school.

The mural has now been painted over, as are many smaller projects in Philadelphia, and that little parcel of grass has been turned into a building. The feeling of accomplishment, of voices heard, of confidence, remains.

The boy who told me I was his favorite teacher asks if it's okay if he spends his lunches with me this year. Asks if I'd like to play *Super Smash Bros*. Asks if he can tell me about his summer.

Of course.

And in the back of my mind, no matter where I go, no matter what I do, I will always hold one image right next to my heart:

Donkey Kong and Kirby, looking at each other, smiling.

The Joy of Diagnosis

Laura Kate Dale

Often, when a parent of an autistic child writes about the day their diagnosis became official, those accounts are, to put it mildly, pretty damned bleak. Stories of mourning a life their child will never get to live, milestones they assume will never be achieved, and a bleak view that their child's life is doomed to be inferior and lesser now that their experience has one of the "scary" labels.

While I can understand, to an extent, that it must be scary as a parent having to reevaluate your expectations for your child's life and future experiences, I find it depressing to see how many parents of autistic children seem ready to write their children off before they've had much of a chance to live that life yet.

I wasn't diagnosed autistic until my late teens, but even so I experienced some of this myself from the people around me. The doctor who gave me my diagnosis was apologetic about the news. When I shared the news with friends and family, I was met with awkward uncertainty, and attempts to make sure I wasn't struggling with the information.

Diagnosis of any kind can be scary, in that sudden changes can be a lot to adjust to, but for me, the day I got my autism diagnosis was one of the most joyful days of my life. To me, it was baffling that nobody else seemed to share my excitement, and my glee, at finally having a name for what I had always been living with.

Without going deep into the specifics, I had really struggled as an undiagnosed autistic child. Sure, part of that struggle was the autism symptoms, the sensory oversensitivity, routine alteration anxiety, and the social isolation. But, perhaps more than anything else, what made life undiagnosed difficult was knowing I was different, and not knowing why.

I can't speak for any other autistic person, but for me, I knew from a pretty young age something about me was different to the people around me. Without a diagnostic label, I tended to absorb the language that my peers, usually my bullies, used to identify what set me apart.

I was weird. I was a handful of ableist slurs. I was broken.

That's why my initial response to getting an autism diagnosis was relief, and a calm wave of joy. Yeah, I had a disability, but that wasn't new. The day I got my diagnosis wasn't the day I became autistic, but it was the day I put a name to the beast. It wasn't the day I became different from my peers, but it was the day I learned that I was not alone, and that other people out there had been through what I was going through. It wasn't the day I started to struggle, but the day I realized there were other people out there, with tools to cope and survive in a difficult world, and I could seek out their advice for ideas on how to live my own life in a way that was less confusing and scary.

My diagnosis was a guiding light that brought me to new information, a kit of helpful supplies to help me navigate the world, and most of all it was proof I wasn't alone and broken, but instead part of a community I had not known could empathize with what I was going through.

While the immediate feeling I had on the day I was diagnosed was relief, over time the exact shape of my feelings about diagnosis shifted a little. While I would generally describe myself as feeling joyous, I won't pretend there weren't moments in there where I struggled. There were moments where I mourned the time lost, and the years I lost to a lack of coping mechanisms, but even those I tried to see the joy within. Sure, I got diagnosed later than I would have liked, but I was also diagnosed earlier than many other people in my life. Instead of mourning the time I lacked support, I tried to make an effort to celebrate the years I got to know and understand myself that not everyone is lucky enough to benefit from.

Where I struggled somewhat at first with feeling limited by my condition, and the areas in which clinicians described me as inferior to my peers, I over time saw ways in which I was unique, and could thrive in my own way.

Going through years of not having a name for my struggles led to a lot of introspection. Once I had a diagnosis, and could plot those introspective thoughts onto something manageable and actionable, I was freed up to create, taking all the words I had spent years keeping bottled up and using them to verbalize experiences I had not seen many others discuss.

Once I started to surround myself with other autistic adults, as well as those sympathetic and willing to learn, I had a shortcut to explain areas where I struggled, and areas where I found joy.

I know people expected me to mourn being diagnosed autistic, but at the end of the day, I felt nothing but joy in the face of my new self-understanding.

A beast is less scary once you know its name, and can see its form in detail. Sometimes, that's enough to make it less scary. Sometimes, it can be a relief just to know it's not only you.

You Have Rainbow Drops

Josephine Baird

Lecturer, writer, artist, and autistic trans woman who lives with her wife and daughter in Sweden.

"Mummy, you have rainbow drops," is what our daughter Miranda told me one sunny afternoon, pointing to my cheek where a tear had rolled down. I had been having a particularly rough time of it, and I was sitting on the couch in our flat, crying. Miranda had seen me and wandered over to make the observation. I understood implicitly what she meant, and it moved me deeply. The phrase would enter into our collective language to express a particular kind of emotion. Because, as it turns out, expressing ourselves is something we prefer to do non-normatively, in part because we are both autistic.

Writing this story, I realize that for most of my life prior to Miranda's birth, I had felt a tremendous lack of words to describe my experiences. Language didn't come easy. I remember being able to reproduce the words, but not really being able to internalize what they "meant" for other people. I always felt like we might be communicating quite different things with the words we used; that we had a different perspective, a different way of being, and a different way of learning. I found that words themselves were inadequate to express that realization.

I mean, how do you use words to explain the feeling that you don't have the words to explain how you are feeling? I remember having the impulse to flap my hands in those moments, an impulse to stim to relieve the tension of not understanding why I was different from what was expected of me. And what made this even harder was how my language and behavior were further limited by propriety, custom, and gender. From the earliest age, according to social rules I never fully understood nor ascribed to, I was expected to express some things and not others, at particular times and not others, in designated places and not others. And it made no sense to me at all. Not least because I didn't feel like the gender my environment kept insisting I was.

I was told I was a boy, and boys were supposed to be aggressive and take up space. They were supposed to be confident and stoic. They weren't supposed to clap and jump when excited, nor rock back and forth when anxious or tired. They weren't supposed to break down in tears of anguish when they didn't understand something or were overwhelmed by the world which felt panic-inducingly alien. Rather, the only term I heard to describe that last behavior was "tantrum"; a word which most certainly didn't communicate what I was actually feeling.

There seemed to be an endless number of unwritten rules, and no language or opportunity to describe my despair at not comprehending them. Because even expressing confusion about the rules was itself also inappropriate. Knowing the rules was supposed to be natural and normal. One is simply aware of them, because that is how we all are. But I didn't know them, and it wasn't how I was.

I exhibited the wrong kind of vulnerability at the wrong time, overshared feelings, misunderstood irony, wasn't able to read the room and not be awkward, and didn't have the words to express my panic and fear. I acted out with clapping, waving, or flapping at inappropriate times. In short, I got it wrong a lot. And when I got it wrong, the punishment was swift and cruel.

So, I learned quickly to pretend I knew the rules, as if I could read people's emotions easily, that the available words were adequate to express myself, that I was a "normal" person who wasn't constantly terrified I would be misunderstood or found out to be anything other than like everyone else. I learned to mask my autism, and for a time, my gender as well. And the most insidious part was that I learned to mask it even to myself.

It took me years to realize that if social rules and behaviors were supposed to be so natural and universal, then why did they need to be policed so fiercely? It took even longer to build confidence enough to break those rules. Eventually I developed a language for my experience, and found a community and family who was generous enough to help me find another way to be.

A big part of that was getting to know our child, learning how she communicated and reflecting that I had often wanted to communicate similarly. And it started by trying to show our daughter that it was okay to be different.

When Miranda was born, I didn't know I was autistic. I had realized I was a woman, and how damaging restricting expression could be. We were determined to make sure that Miranda would not have the same kind of limiting experience I had growing up. We collectively agreed that she would be given the opportunity and space to express herself as she needed to.

To make sure she knew she could, we figured it wasn't enough to say that she could. It was critical to also model that behavior in ourselves. I knew from personal experience how painful and confusing it was to be told "You can be whatever you want to be," and then realize how untrue that was when you saw what people actually let you do and be.

I guess that's why expressing myself freely was hard for me at first. Because despite coming out as queer, and learning to embrace difference, I was still suppressing my autistic behaviors. I was hiding them from everyone, including myself. I did have a sense that I was still hiding parts of myself, even if I didn't quite know what or why. I was determined to express myself more freely for Miranda, who was growing up at an alarming rate, as children tend to do. Though, not in a way that children typically do.

One of the first indications of this was that she didn't start to verbally communicate at the age you might expect. We took her to see people who could help us learn how to support her and we came to understand that Miranda was "atypically autistic." Which means that she is autistic, but also atypically so. And part of that meant she learned and expressed in different ways. That included language, and communicating in general.

We spent the following years being guided by Miranda on how to support her learning and communication. At first, we tried sign language, which proved popular, if not entirely successful. She seemed to enjoy the exuberance for gesture, something I recognized in myself but still didn't realize why. In the end, she learned spoken language by repeating terms and phrases she heard from different places and understood to mean things close to her experience. The phrases she chose were from her favorite sources, like cartoons she liked, or conversations we had with her that she enjoyed.

I realized that I understood her choices quickly; the way she would use generic words to refer to a breadth of meaning. It made perfect sense to me that the word "cookie" could refer to any kind of food and the phrase "don't be disappointed, try again" could mean anything from "don't worry," to "let's give it another go." Eventually, she began to form her own sentences in the way she understood them, which included metaphors and similes to explain anything she didn't feel she had a word for. For example, she called a helium-filled balloon a "balloon with clouds in." Again, I found her way of communicating to make perfect sense. I recognized it from the time in my life when I found words to be inadequate, but unlike her, I hadn't had the opportunity to try to find my own way with them.

For others though, her particular way of describing the world could be challenging. But we were keen to let her develop the way she needed to, and her communication style seemed rich, creative, and perfectly functional. She came to use a combination of normative verbal communication, something she is quite adept at in both English and Swedish. Nonetheless, despite her wide vocabulary, she still finds reason to use her own metaphors and terminology to describe those things she sees differently or finds language inadequate to describe, which often includes emotions.

Feelings proved to be challenging for her to express verbally, especially when she was younger. These were immensely frustrating times for her, finding that she wasn't able to express her feelings to us in the way she wanted. My wife experimented with a way of asking her what color her emotions were and where in her body she felt them. This proved to be very useful, and we soon realized how much she appreciated using metaphor to communicate. She adopted the terminology, and would mix colors and locations of feelings to express complex or conflicting emotions.

So, now, when she is older and knows the normative words for feelings, it can still be easier for her to explain to us what colors the emotion is and where it is within her. This is especially true for "big emotions," which was the term she chose for intense or overwhelming feelings. It was when I realized I understood her choice of language implicitly, and how it mirrored my own impulses, that I should have perhaps realized I might be autistic too. But that took encouragement from my wife.

An autistic friend had pointed out to me one day that I had many of the qualities that an autistic person might have. Certain confusions and anxieties about people and the social world, a particular affinity for routines and rules, aversions to certain sounds, and a joy at special interests which I could focus on intently. I disagreed and said that many of the qualities she had noticed could be because of post-traumatic stress disorder (PTSD), which was something I already knew I had.

I told my wife about the conversation, and she agreed with my friend, and that she had thought the same for some time, in part because of the way I implicitly understood and communicated with Miranda.

I still couldn't quite take it in. There were so many other explanations for my anxieties and behavior. I had PTSD. I am a trans woman married to another woman, in a society that can be hostile to being those kinds of non-normative. But, the more I thought about it, the more my wife's comments resonated. I decided to get assessed, to perhaps learn something about myself. What I wasn't prepared for was how much joy it would bring me as well.

I was nervous about it though. Authorities and institutions scare me in lots of ways. We worked very hard to shield Miranda from those that could be especially problematic, and sought out only those who had strong backgrounds of working with autistic people and thus would be positive in their support. I didn't quite know how to do that for myself.

But I was lucky. I met a very nice man who ran exercises with me, asked me a bunch of questions, and finally told me that, yes, I was autistic. He helped me to understand that though some of my social anxiety came from PTSD, plenty also came from not understanding others implicitly and finding it difficult to reproduce social norms and communicate like others.

He helped me to consider that my failure to express these normativities had been part of the social circumstances that led to my PTSD. He helped me realize that the mask I presented to the world wasn't just a way of protecting myself from attack as a queer person, but also allowed me to shut away my natural autistic behaviors. A mask I had used to hide my constant fear that I would be misunderstood and how I often misunderstood others.

But there were people I did implicitly understand—my non-normative and neurodiverse friends and family. And that was when it dawned on me. I understood Miranda's way of communicating because, for me, normative language was inadequate too. I had never found the words to express how I felt and thought. I hadn't been allowed to stim or express in any other way. But I had been trying to find ways to communicate anyway for much of my life. I had been a dancer because movement could express things there was no verbal language for. As a visual artist, I found meaning in composition and color. As a game designer, I learned that interactivity could lead to creative and embodied comprehensions. Each of these arts provided me another language, another way to communicate and understand others. And each was a special interest that brought me elation and satisfaction.

I cried with joy in my assessment when I was given explicit permission to express myself and to take off the mask I had been wearing for so long. I was asked about my impulse to flap and clap. I was asked, very simply, what I would do if I didn't have to worry about how it looked to others. I said that I wanted to shake my hands in the air and clap in front of me. He suggested I try, and when I did, I cried from the release and joy of it.

I find myself crying now, remembering the moment and writing it down. The sudden burst of color and light that came into me when I let go was stunning. I had spent a lifetime stopping myself from doing that in front of anyone, including myself. In that moment, I realized what it meant to express and communicate this way, to others and to myself. It was a physical expression which made me feel better when things were overwhelming. And it was a way to communicate my excitement and joy to others.

When I flap and clap now, it is sometimes because I am anxious but it is also often because I am joyful.

I re-acquired a language that was beyond words and social norms, which unlike those things, actually did feel intrinsically comprehensible. Normal and natural. For me. And for Miranda. And others too. And when I realized that, I felt a joy in the sense of commonality. Because even though my being autistic is not the same as others' experience of being autistic, I felt like I could intrinsically understand the wish to express ourselves without the hindrances that societies can place on us.

And that is how I understood immediately what Miranda meant when she said I had "rainbow drops." The sun was shining that day and she had been enjoying the refracted colors that splayed out on the floor from light passing through the crystals we had hanging in the window. When she came close to my face, I realized she was looking at my cheeks very closely and had craned her head to look through the tears, making the connection between light refracting through the crystal and through the drops. And furthermore, she thought it was beautiful.

When I understood that, I started to cry more, but not because I was sad, but instead because I felt we could communicate something beyond the words themselves. I felt like I could share my feelings more profoundly and completely, both sad and joyful, with my daughter. And we now had a new term for tears that we still use to this day.